2020 Cumulative Supplement to

Arrest, Search, and Investigation in North Carolina

Robert L. Farb and Christopher Tyner

The School of Government at the University of North Carolina at Chapel Hill works to improve the lives of North Carolinians by engaging in practical scholarship that helps public officials and citizens understand and improve state and local government. Established in 1931 as the Institute of Government, the School provides educational, advisory, and research services for state and local governments. The School of Government is also home to a nationally ranked Master of Public Administration program, the North Carolina Judicial College, and specialized centers focused on community and economic development, information technology, and environmental finance.

As the largest university-based local government training, advisory, and research organization in the United States, the School of Government offers up to 200 courses, webinars, and specialized conferences for more than 12,000 public officials each year. In addition, faculty members annually publish approximately 50 books, manuals, reports, articles, bulletins, and other print and online content related to state and local government. The School also produces the *Daily Bulletin Online* each day the General Assembly is in session, reporting on activities for members of the legislature and others who need to follow the course of legislation.

Operating support for the School of Government's programs and activities comes from many sources, including state appropriations, local government membership dues, private contributions, publication sales, course fees, and service contracts.

Visit sog.unc.edu or call 919.966.5381 for more information on the School's courses, publications, programs, and services.

Michael R. Smith, DEAN
Aimee N. Wall, SENIOR ASSOCIATE DEAN
Jen Willis, ASSOCIATE DEAN FOR DEVELOPMENT
Michael Vollmer, ASSOCIATE DEAN FOR ADMINISTRATION

FACULTY

Whitney Afonso
Trey Allen
Gregory S. Allison
Lydian Altman
David N. Ammons
Maureen Berner
Frayda S. Bluestein
Kirk Boone
Mark F. Botts
Anita R. Brown-Graham
Peg Carlson
Connor Crews
Leisha DeHart-Davis
Shea Riggsbee Denning
Sara DePasquale
Jacquelyn Greene

Margaret F. Henderson
Norma Houston
Cheryl Daniels Howell
Willow S. Jacobson
Robert P. Joyce
Diane M. Juffras
Dona G. Lewandowski
Adam Lovelady
James M. Markham
Christopher B. McLaughlin
Kara A. Millonzi
Jill D. Moore
Jonathan Q. Morgan
Ricardo S. Morse
C. Tyler Mulligan
Kimberly L. Nelson

David W. Owens
William C. Rivenbark
Dale J. Roenigk
John Rubin
Jessica Smith
Meredith Smith
Carl W. Stenberg III
John B. Stephens
Charles Szypszak
Thomas H. Thornburg
Shannon H. Tufts
Jeffrey B. Welty (on leave)
Richard B. Whisnant
Brittany L. Williams

Contents

Chapter 2 Appendix: Case Summaries   13

Arrests, Investigative Stops, and Related Issues   13

Chapter 3

Law of Search and Seizure   33

Chapter 3 Appendix: Case Summaries   39

Search and Seizure Issues   39

Chapter 4

Search Warrants, Administrative Inspection Warrants, and Nontestimonial Identification Orders   57

Chapter 5

Interrogation and Confessions, Lineups and Other Identification Procedures, and Undercover Officers and Informants   79

Preface

This 2020 cumulative supplement updates the fifth edition of *Arrest, Search, and Investigation in North Carolina* (UNC School of Government, 2016). It includes the contents of the 2018 cumulative supplement to the fifth edition, so that cumulative supplement is no longer needed.

The supplement is current through July 1, 2020, encompassing the session laws of the North Carolina General Assembly and cases of the United States Supreme Court, North Carolina appellate courts, and the Fourth Circuit Court of Appeals. Note, however, that the state legislature is likely to meet in additional 2020 sessions after July 1.

This supplement, just like the 2018 supplement, does not include any content concerning two brief chapters of the fifth edition: Chapter 1 (An Introduction to Constitutional Law and North Carolina Criminal Law and Procedure) and Chapter 6 (Rules of Evidence in Criminal Cases).

Thanks to the many School of Government colleagues who wrote many of the case summaries in this supplement or reviewed, edited, or prepared the supplement for publication.

We welcome comments about the structure or content of this supplement or the fifth edition. We may be reached at farb@sog.unc.edu and ctyner@sog.unc.edu, respectively.

Robert L. Farb
Christopher Tyner
Chapel Hill
July 2020

Chapter 2

Law of Arrest and Investigative Stops

Jurisdiction (page 14)
Limits on Law Enforcement Officers' Jurisdiction (page 14)
Territorial Jurisdiction (page 14)
Company police officers (page 15)

Legislation enacted in 2017[1] amended Section 6 of Chapter 74E of the North Carolina General Statutes (hereinafter G.S.) by adding two new subsections. One of the new subsections permits company police agencies to enter into mutual aid agreements with municipalities and counties to the same extent as municipal police departments pursuant to Chapter 160A of the General Statutes.[2] The other permits company police officers to provide temporary assistance to a law enforcement agency at the request of that agency, or the head of the agency's designee, regardless of whether a mutual aid agreement is in place.[3] The statute states that while providing temporary assistance to a law enforcement agency, a company police officer has the same powers vested in law enforcement officers of the agency asking for assistance, but that nothing in the statute expands a company police officer's authority to initiate or conduct an independent investigation into violations of criminal laws outside the scope of the company police officer's subject matter or territorial jurisdiction.[4]

Subject-Matter Jurisdiction (page 18)
Alcohol law enforcement agents (page 18)

Legislation enacted in 2019[5] relocated the Alcohol Law Enforcement (ALE) branch of the State Bureau of Investigation to a division of the Department of Public Safety. Formerly, the primary responsibility of ALE agents was to enforce Alcoholic Beverage Control (ABC), lottery, and youth tobacco laws, but they also had authority to arrest and take other enforcement actions for any criminal offense. The 2019 legislation specified that ALE agents have authority over criminal offenses in certain circumstances, such as offenses on the premises of, or elsewhere when related to locations holding a permit from, the ABC Commission or Education Lottery Commission; offenses occurring in the agents' presence; and crimes of violence or breaches of the peace. The agents' primary responsibility remains enforcement of ABC laws; lottery laws; youth tobacco laws; and lottery, gaming, bingo, and raffle laws.

Special Jurisdictional Issues (page 20)
Immigration enforcement by North Carolina law enforcement officers (page 20)

Add the following text to footnote 68: In *Chavez v. McFadden*, 374 N.C. 458 (2020), the North Carolina Supreme Court ruled that state judicial officials acting in counties in which the sheriff has entered a § 287(g) agreement with the federal government do not have the authority to grant applications to issue writs of habeas corpus for and to order the release of inmates held pursuant to immigration-related arrest warrants

---

1. S.L. 2017-57, § 17.2.(a).
2. G.S. 74E-6(h).
3. G.S. 74E-6(i).
4. *Id.*
5. S.L. 2019-203, effective October 1, 2019.

and detainers (§ 287(g) of the Immigration and Nationality Act is codified at 8 U.S.C. § 1357(g)). Thus, it ruled that the trial court erred by ordering the release of two inmates who were being held under a claim of federal authority that the trial court was required to respect.

Areas controlled by the federal government (page 20)

In footnote 72 on page 22, there is a discussion of the special jurisdictional issues involving the Cherokee Indian Reservation. Add the following case: State v. Nobles, 373 N.C. 471 (2020) (the defendant was convicted in state court of various offenses; the court rejected the defendant's challenge to the jurisdiction of state court on the ground that he was an "Indian" under the federal Indian Major Crimes Act and thus was subject to exclusive federal criminal jurisdiction; the court also ruled that the trial court did not err in not requiring a special jury verdict on this legal jurisdictional issue when there was no factual dispute to resolve.

Expanded Jurisdiction through Cooperating Law Enforcement Agencies (page 24)

Legislation enacted in 2018[6] amended G.S. 160A-288 and 160A-288.2 to create, in the legislation's words, "a presumption that allows one law enforcement agency to easily assist another law enforcement agency whenever necessary." Under amended G.S. 160A-288, the head of any law enforcement agency may temporarily provide assistance to another agency in enforcing North Carolina law if such assistance is requested in writing by the head of the requesting agency, unless doing so is specifically prohibited or limited by an officially adopted ordinance of the city or county of the assisting agency. Such assistance may include allowing officers of the assisting agency to work temporarily with officers of the requesting agency and lending equipment and supplies. Amended G.S. 160A-288.2 allows assistance to be provided by a local law enforcement agency to a state law enforcement agency under analogous circumstances. Prior to the 2018 legislative amendments, each statute stated that such assistance could be provided "in accordance with rules, policies, or guidelines" adopted by the city or county of the assisting agency.

Legislation enacted in 2019[7] amended G.S. 160A-288 to authorize mutual aid agreements with out-of-state law enforcement agencies if the law of the other state allows for mutual aid with out-of-state law enforcement officers.

Legal Standards (page 26)

Introduction (page 26)

The fifth paragraph of this section of the main text discusses the wide variety of interactions officers have with people and, among other things, explains that officers do not seize a person merely by approaching him or her in a public place and asking questions if the person is willing to answer. In *State v. Wilson*,[8] the North Carolina Court of Appeals held that a seizure did not occur when an officer went to a residence to find a man subject to outstanding arrest warrants and waved his hands to tell the driver of a pickup truck leaving the residence to stop so that the officer could ask the driver about the man subject to the outstanding warrants. The officer had no suspicion that the driver was the man subject to the warrants or that the driver was engaged in criminal activity; the officer did not have his weapon drawn and had not activated the lights or siren on his patrol car nor used it to block the road. When the defendant stopped the vehicle, the officer almost immediately smelled an odor of alcohol from inside the vehicle. After the defendant admitted that he had been drinking, the officer arrested the defendant for impaired driving. The court held that because a

---

6. S.L. 2018-87.

7. S.L. 2019-130, effective July 19, 2019.

8. 250 N.C. App. 781 (2016), *aff'd per curiam*, 370 N.C. 389 (2017).

reasonable person would have felt free to decline the officer's request to stop, no seizure occurred; rather, the encounter was a consensual one. The North Carolina Supreme Court affirmed this ruling on appeal.[9]

The same paragraph of the main text explains that a formal arrest for a criminal offense clearly is a Fourth Amendment seizure. The North Carolina Court of Appeals also has held that a seizure occurs, at least in some circumstances, when an officer takes a publicly intoxicated person to jail for the purpose of assisting the person pursuant to the authority of G.S. 122C-303.[10] That statute authorizes an officer to "assist an individual found intoxicated in a public place by directing or transporting that individual to a city or county jail," but provides that such assistance may be rendered only "if the intoxicated individual is apparently in need of and apparently unable to provide for himself food, clothing, or shelter but is not apparently in need of immediate medical care and if no other facility is readily available to receive him."[11] In *State v. Burwell*, the court stated that "taking an individual to jail under [G.S. 122C-303] against his will constitutes an arrest,"[12] but seemed to suggest that an arrest would not occur if the requirements of the statute were otherwise satisfied and the intoxicated person consented to being taken to jail.[13]

Footnote 101 (page 26)
Additional cases for this footnote: State v. Turnage, 259 N.C. App. 719 (2018) (the trial court erred by concluding that a seizure occurred when a detective activated his blue lights upon encountering a van that was stopped in the middle of the road for unknown reasons and that fled as the detective approached the van; the court of appeals explained that the defendant, who was driving the van, did not yield to the detective's show of authority until she discontinued fleeing and her further movement was prevented by an officer's patrol vehicle used to block the van at an intersection; because the defendant was not seized upon activation of the blue lights, the defendant's criminal activity observed by the detective between the activation of the blue lights and the conclusion of the chase justified the defendant's arrest); State v. Mangum, 250 N.C. App. 714 (2016) (because the defendant did not stop his vehicle when an officer activated his blue lights and bumped his siren, circumstances that the officer observed between the activation of the blue lights and the time when the defendant stopped his vehicle were properly considered by the trial court in its reasonable suspicion inquiry; the court noted that the defendant's failure to yield to the officer's show of authority for two minutes was itself a circumstance that added to the suspicion of criminal activity); State v. Mahatha, ___ N.C. App. ___, 832 S.E.2d 914 (2019) (similar ruling, citing *Mangum*, above).[14]

---

9. *Id. See* Shea Denning, *State v. Wilson: Was the Defendant Seized When He Stopped Upon the Officer's Signal?*, UNC SCH. OF GOV'T: N.C. CRIM. L. BLOG (Dec. 14, 2016), https://www.sog.unc.edu/blogs/nc-criminal-law/state-v-wilson-was-defendant-seized-when-he-stopped-upon-officer%E2%80%99s-signal.

10. State v. Burwell, 256 N.C. App. 722 (2017); Davis v. Town of S. Pines, 116 N.C. App. 663 (1994).

11. G.S. 122C-303.

12. 256 N.C. App. at 732. The court of appeals stated the same principle in *Davis*, 116 N.C. App. at 671.

13. *Burwell*, 256 N.C. App. at 732.

14. For a discussion of *Turnage*, see Shea Denning, *State v. Turnage and Determining When a Defendant Is Seized*, UNC SCH. OF GOV'T: N.C. CRIM. L. BLOG (May 23, 2018), https://www.sog.unc.edu/blogs/nc-criminal-law/state-v-turnage-and-determining-when-defendant-seized. For a discussion of *Mangum*, see Bob Farb, *When Does a Seizure Occur When an Officer's Vehicle Displays Emergency Lights That Direct a Vehicle to Stop?*, UNC SCH. OF GOV'T: N.C. CRIM. L. BLOG (Mar. 28, 2017), https://nccriminallaw.sog.unc.edu/seizure-occur-officers-vehicle-displays-emergency-lights-directs-vehicle-stop/.

Officer's Objectively Reasonable Mistake of Fact or Law in Determining Reasonable Suspicion or Probable Cause (page 28)

In *Kansas v. Glover*[15] the United States Supreme Court ruled that when a law enforcement officer knows that the registered owner of a vehicle has a revoked driver's license and lacks information negating an inference that the owner is the driver of the vehicle, a traffic stop is supported by reasonable suspicion and does not violate the Fourth Amendment.

In *State v. Eldridge*,[16] the North Carolina Court of Appeals held that an officer's mistake of law was not objectively reasonable and, consequently, a traffic stop based upon that mistake of law was not supported by reasonable suspicion. In *Eldridge*, an officer stopped a vehicle registered in Tennessee for driving without a mirror on the driver's side of the vehicle based on his genuine but mistaken belief that G.S. 20-126(b), which requires such a mirror on vehicles registered in North Carolina, applied to the defendant's vehicle. This case provided the court of appeals its first opportunity to apply *Heien v. North Carolina*, 574 U.S. 54 (2014), a case discussed in the main text. Reviewing the application of *Heien* in other jurisdictions, the court stated that those cases "establish that in order for an officer's mistake of law while enforcing a statute to be objectively reasonable, the statute at issue must be ambiguous."[17] The court also noted that some courts in other jurisdictions "have further required that there be an absence of settled caselaw interpreting the statute at issue in order for the officer's mistake of law to be deemed objectively reasonable."[18] Distinguishing G.S. 20-126(b) from the statute at issue in *Heien*, the court said that the text of G.S. 20-126(b) is "clear and unambiguous" and, thus, "a reasonable officer reading this statute would understand the requirement that a vehicle be equipped with a driver's side exterior mirror does not apply to vehicles that—like Defendant's vehicle—are registered in another state."[19] Because the officer's mistake of law was not objectively reasonable, the stop was not supported by reasonable suspicion.[20]

The Authority to Make an Investigative Stop: Reasonable Suspicion (page 29)

Determination of Reasonable Suspicion (page 30)

The final paragraph of this section of the main text discusses common misunderstandings about the legal grounds to make investigative stops of drivers for motor vehicle violations. In *State v. Johnson*,[21] the North Carolina Supreme Court took time to correct what it saw as a misunderstanding in the court of appeals opinion regarding the grounds for making a traffic stop and explicitly emphasized an inherent and invariable quality of reasonable suspicion implicit in the main text and relevant court opinions—that reasonable suspicion is a standard less stringent than a legal certainty. The court explained that while observing an actual traffic violation is a sufficient basis for a stop,[22] such an observation is not necessary and "[t]o meet the reasonable suspicion standard, it is enough for the officer to *reasonably believe* that a driver has violated the law."[23]

---

15. 589 U.S. ___, 140 S. Ct. 1183 (2020).

16. 249 N.C. App. 493 (2016).

17. *Id.* at 499.

18. *Id.*

19. *Id.* at 500.

20. For a discussion of *Eldridge*, see Bob Farb, *An Officer's Reasonable Mistake of Law and Recent Court of Appeals Ruling*, UNC SCH. OF GOV'T: N.C. CRIM. L. BLOG (Sept. 27, 2016), https://nccriminallaw.sog.unc.edu/officers-reasonable-mistake-law-recent-court-appeals-ruling/.

21. 370 N.C. 32 (2017).

22. For recent cases illustrating this point, see *State v. Sutton*, 259 N.C. App. 891 (2018) (explaining that when an officer actually observes a traffic violation, it is a "bright line rule" that an officer may conduct a stop on the basis of that observation), and *State v. Jones*, 258 N.C. App. 643 (2018) (an officer's observation of a single instance of a vehicle crossing the double yellow centerline in violation of state motor vehicle law provided reasonable suspicion to support a traffic stop). For a discussion of *Sutton* and *Jones*, see Shea Denning, *A Bright Line Rule for Traffic Stops*, UNC SCH. OF GOV'T: N.C. CRIM. L. BLOG (June 20, 2018), https://nccriminallaw.sog.unc.edu/a-bright-line-rule-for-traffic-stops/.

23. *Johnson*, 370 N.C. at 38 (emphasis in original).

Appellate Court Cases on Reasonable Suspicion (page 31)

The first case discussed in this section of the main text is *Navarette v. California*,[24] in which the United States Supreme Court held that an officer had reasonable suspicion to stop a vehicle based on a 911 call reporting dangerous driving. On page 107 of the appendix case summaries relevant to this section of the main text is a summary of *State v. Blankenship*,[25] a pre-*Navarette* case also involving a 911 call of dangerous driving leading to a vehicle stop. A relatively recent North Carolina Court of Appeals case in the same vein as *Navarette* and *Blankenship* is *State v. Walker*.[26] In *Walker*, the court of appeals held that an informant-driver's tip relayed to highway patrol dispatch and thereafter to a state trooper reporting that another driver was driving dangerously while drinking a beer did not provide reasonable suspicion to stop the defendant. The non-anonymous informant-driver reported that another driver traveling along U.S. 258 was driving at speeds of approximately 80–100 m.p.h., was drinking a beer, was driving "very erratically," and almost ran the informant off the road "a few times." At some point, though it was unclear whether before or after the stop was initiated, the vehicle in question was described as a "gray Ford passenger vehicle."[27] Noting that the informant-driver was unable to specifically identify the vehicle in question because it was out of sight and that the trooper did not corroborate the tip by witnessing any erratic driving similar to that described by the informant, the court held that the tip "did not have enough indicia of credibility to create reasonable suspicion for the Trooper to stop Defendant's vehicle."[28] It appears that the informant-driver's inability to specifically identify the vehicle in question, a factor that distinguishes the case from *Navarette*, had significant influence on the *Walker* court's determination that the stop was not supported by reasonable suspicion.

In *State v. Nicholson*,[29] the North Carolina Supreme Court, reversing the court of appeals, held that reasonable suspicion supported an officer's investigative stop of the defendant. While on patrol at 4:00 a.m., an officer encountered a car parked in a turn lane next to a gas station with its headlights on but no turn signal blinking. Upon pulling his patrol vehicle next to the stopped car, the officer observed two men in the car, one in the driver's seat and the other, the defendant, sitting directly behind him in the back seat. The defendant appeared to be pulling a mask over his face but pushed it back up when he saw the officer. The officer asked the men, who said they were brothers, whether they were okay; each said yes, but the driver made a hand motion at his neck area. The officer then parked at the gas station and continued to observe the car, which did not move or display a turn signal. The officer then approached the car again. As he approached, the defendant exited the car and the driver began edging the car forward. The officer again asked if everything was okay, and though the driver again said yes, he shook his head "no." As the officer asked again about the situation, the driver interjected that everything was fine but that he had to get to work and the officer told him to go. After the driver left, the officer asked the defendant, who wanted to walk to the gas station, to "hang tight" and asked if he had any weapons. Taking account of the totality of the circumstances, the court determined that reasonable suspicion supported the officer's seizure of the defendant by asking him to "hang tight" and asking whether he had weapons. According to the court, the facts "strongly suggested that [the driver] had been under threat from defendant, as well as the possibility that defendant was in the process of robbing [the driver]."[30] Finding that the court of appeals placed undue weight on the officer's subjective interpretation of the facts, the supreme court emphasized that the reasonable suspicion analysis is an objective inquiry.

---

24. 572 U.S. 393 (2014).
25. 230 N.C. App. 113 (2013).
26. 255 N.C. App. 828 (2017).
27. *Id.* at 829.
28. *Id.* at 836.
29. 371 N.C. 284 (2018).
30. *Id.* at 290.

The Authority to Arrest: Probable Cause (page 39)
Determination of Probable Cause with or without an Arrest Warrant (page 40)
Appellate Court Cases on Probable Cause (page 41)

In *District of Columbia v. Wesby*,[31] the United States Supreme Court reversed the D.C. circuit and held that officers had probable cause to arrest several people for the offense of unauthorized entry where the officers discovered the people at a raucous party at an unoccupied house. Officers responding to a noise complaint regarding a house that the caller said had been vacant for several months immediately observed that the interior of the house was in disarray and looked like a vacant property. The officers smelled marijuana and observed beer bottles and cups of liquor on the floor. There was hardly any furniture in the house, and the living room appeared to have been converted into a makeshift strip club. Several women giving lap dances while partygoers looked on were wearing only bras and thongs, with cash tucked into their garter belts. Some partygoers scattered upon seeing the uniformed officers. A naked woman and several men were found in an upstairs bedroom with a bare mattress on the floor and multiple open condom wrappers. Many partygoers claimed they were invited to the house to attend a bachelor party, but no one could identify the bachelor. Officers eventually spoke to a person on the phone who claimed that she was renting the house and had given her permission for the party, but officers thereafter spoke to the owner of the house who said that a rental agreement had not been reached and that no one had permission to use the house. The officers then arrested twenty-one partygoers for unlawful entry. Stating that the D.C. circuit engaged in an "excessively technical dissection" of the factors relevant to probable cause, the Supreme Court faulted the lower panel for conducting an analysis that viewed each fact in isolation and dismissed individual circumstances susceptible of innocent explanation. Citing its precedents, the Court explained that a proper analysis of probable cause requires consideration of "the whole picture" and the "degree of suspicion" attached to particular acts that are suspicious even if not themselves criminal offenses. Under this analysis, the Court found that "[t]he circumstances here certainly suggested criminal activity"[32] and provided probable cause for the arrests.

Pretextual Arrest, Investigative Stop, or Search (page 44)

The main text explains that under *United States v. Whren*,[33] an officer may make an arrest or conduct a stop as a pretext to accomplish some other purpose unrelated to the arrest or stop so long as the arrest or stop has a lawful basis. The main text gives the example of a drug investigator conducting a traffic stop on the basis of an observed traffic violation not because of concern with the traffic violation but because the investigator wishes to conduct a drug investigation during the course of the stop. The discussion in the main text continues to accurately reflect the law of pretextual stops generally, but the United States Supreme Court's decision in *Rodriguez v. United States*[34] significantly limits the scope of investigative activities unrelated to the legal basis for a stop that an officer may undertake. Thus, *Rodriguez* affects pretextual stops as a practical matter. *Rodriguez* is discussed in more detail on page 48 of the main text, below in this supplement, and in a recent School of Government publication dealing specifically with North Carolina traffic stops.[35]

---

31. 583 U.S. ___, 138 S. Ct. 577 (2018).

32. *Id.* at ___, 138 S. Ct. at 589.

33. 517 U.S. 806 (1996).

34. 575 U.S. 348 (2015).

35. Shea Riggsbee Denning, Christopher Tyner, & Jeffrey B. Welty, Pulled Over: The Law of Traffic Stops and Offenses in North Carolina 60–61 (UNC School of Government, 2017).

Special Aspects of Stopping Authority (page 46)
Investigative Stop Based on Reasonable Suspicion (page 46)
Length of Time Allowed for an Investigative Stop (page 46)
United States Supreme Court case on delay after completed traffic stop (page 48)

This section of the main text discusses the United States Supreme Court decision in *Rodriguez v. United States*,[36] when the Court held that a "stop exceeding the time needed to handle the matter for which the stop was made violates the Constitution's shield against unreasonable seizures." The North Carolina appellate courts have applied *Rodriguez* or otherwise analyzed cases dealing with the length of time allowed for an investigative stop on several occasions subsequent to the publication of the main text. [37]

In *State v. Reed*,[38] the North Carolina Supreme Court ruled, distinguishing its prior ruling in *State v. Bullock*,[39] discussed below, that a state trooper (Lamm) who stopped a speeding rental car prolonged the stop without having the defendant's voluntary consent or reasonable suspicion of criminal activity. There were two people in the car, the male defendant-driver and a female passenger who rented the vehicle. Lamm had the defendant sit in his patrol car while he checked the status of the rental car and asked some questions about his travel plans. After about twenty minutes and upon confirming that the rental car matter was in order, Lamm returned all paperwork to the defendant and told the defendant that the stop had ended but then said, "I'm going to ask you a few more questions if it is okay with you." Lamm asked the defendant for consent to search the vehicle, to which he replied, "you could break the car down" but then further explained that the trooper should seek consent from the female passenger because she had rented the car. Lamm told the defendant to "sit tight" in the patrol car as he went to confer with her in the rental car. A backup trooper (Ellerbe), who had arrived since the stop had occurred, stationed himself outside the door of Lamm's patrol car while the defendant remained in the passenger seat with the door closed. Lamm obtained consent to search from the female passenger, and cocaine was discovered in the rental car. The court found that trooper Lamm's conduct was authorized by *Bullock* up to his unequivocal statement to the defendant that the traffic stop had been concluded. However, the traffic stop after this point became unlawful under *Rodriguez* because the trooper "prolonged it beyond the time reasonably required to complete its mission."[40] And the defendant was unconstitutionally detained beyond the announced end of the traffic stop because reasonable suspicion did not exist to justify the defendant's further detention (see the court's discussion of the facts involving the reasonable suspicion issue). The court also rejected the State's argument that the defendant consented to prolonging the traffic stop, relying in significant part on Trooper Lamm's telling the defendant to "sit tight" in the trooper's vehicle and Trooper Ellerbe's standing by the door where the defendant was seated.

In *State v. Bullock*,[41] an officer with experience on his department's drug interdiction team pulled the defendant over after observing him speeding, following a truck too closely, and weaving over the white line marking the edge of the road. In the course of the stop, the officer asked the defendant to exit his car and sit in the officer's patrol car, telling him that he would be receiving a warning rather than a ticket. Noting that an officer may order a driver of a lawfully stopped car to exit his vehicle as a matter of course,[42] the North Carolina Supreme Court determined that any amount of time added to the stop by asking the defendant to exit his car "was simply time spent pursuing the mission of the stop."[43] The officer also frisked the defendant for weapons

---

36. 575 U.S. 348, 350 (2015).

37. In addition to the discussion here, see the appendix for other North Carolina appellate cases on this issue as well as Denning, Tyner, & Welty, *supra* note 35, at 60–61.

38. 373 N.C. 498 (2020).

39. 370 N.C. 256 (2017).

40. *Id.* at 511.

41. 370 N.C. 256 (2017).

42. The main text discusses this general rule on page 49.

43. *Bullock*, 370 N.C. at 261–62.

before the defendant entered the officer's patrol car. The court ruled that this frisk did not unconstitutionally prolong the stop for two independent reasons. First, the frisk enhanced the officer's safety and, the court said, "time devoted to officer safety is time that is reasonably required to complete" the mission of the stop.[44] As a second basis for the constitutionality of the frisk, the court determined that the eight or nine seconds required for the frisk did not measurably extend the duration of the stop. The court also determined that the officer's questioning of the defendant during the time required to run database checks related to the mission of the stop did not unlawfully extend the stop because the checks had to be run before the stop could be finished. The court stated the rule of *Rodriguez* as follows: "Under *Rodriguez*, the duration of a traffic stop must be limited to the length of time that is reasonably necessary to accomplish the mission of the stop, unless reasonable suspicion of another crime arose before that mission was completed."[45] The court went on to explain that the "reasonable duration of a traffic stop . . . includes more than just the time needed to write a ticket" and that ordinary inquiries incident to the stop are part of an officer's mission.[46] The court identified driver's license and warrant checks as well as registration and insurance checks as among such ordinary inquiries.[47] The court also added that precautions related to officer safety, including criminal history checks, are within the mission of a traffic stop.[48] Finally, the court noted that investigations into unrelated crimes, even absent reasonable suspicion, are permitted if those investigations do not extend the duration of the stop.[49]

In *State v. Campola*,[50] the North Carolina Court of Appeals reiterated many of the points made by the state supreme court in *Bullock*. Consistent with *Rodriguez* and *Bullock*, the court stated that "database searches of driver's licenses, warrants, vehicle registrations, and proof of insurance all fall within the mission of a traffic stop" and also explained that criminal history checks were permissible officer safety precautions within the mission of the stop.[51] The court said that the stopping officer's request for backup, made because there were two occupants in the vehicle, also was a permissible safety precaution.[52]

Footnote 201 (page 48)

The main text associated with footnote 201 explains that *Rodriguez* does not alter the general rule that an officer may lawfully extend a completed traffic stop if the officer develops reasonable suspicion of other criminal activity while otherwise diligently pursuing the mission of the stop, and the footnote itself provides examples of post-*Rodriguez* North Carolina appellate cases to that effect. Additional cases for this footnote include: State v. Downey, 370 N.C. 507 (2018) (reasonable suspicion supported extension of stop); State v. Bullock, 370 N.C. 256 (2017) (same); State v. Sutton, 259 N.C. App. 891 (2018) (same); State v. Cox, 259 N.C. App. 650 (2018) (same); State v. Campola, 258 N.C. App. 292 (2018) (same). *But see* State v. Reed, 373 N.C. 498 (2020) (reasonable suspicion did not exist to extend completed traffic stop), discussed in the text above.

Scope of Investigative Stop: Investigative Techniques (page 49)

Ordering driver and passengers out of vehicle (page 49)

The main text explains that the United States Supreme Court has ruled that an officer who has lawfully stopped a vehicle may order the driver and passengers out of the vehicle without showing any reason to do so under the Fourth Amendment. The North Carolina Supreme Court explicitly recognized an officer's continued authority to do so in *State v. Bullock*.[53]

---

44. *Id*. at 262.
45. *Id*. at 257.
46. *Id*.
47. *Id*.
48. *Id*.
49. *Id*.
50. 258 N.C. App. 292 (2018).
51. *Id*. at 300.
52. *Id*. at 301.
53. 370 N.C. 256 (driver).

Checking Division of Criminal Information or other information source (page 51)

The main text explains that after stopping a suspect, an officer may check for outstanding warrants and other criminally related information if the check does not unduly prolong the stop. In the context of lawful traffic stops, the North Carolina Supreme Court stated that it appeared, based on a decision of the United States Supreme Court, that conducting a criminal history check is an appropriate officer safety precaution inherent in the mission of a traffic stop.[54] Thus, in the context of traffic stops, it appears that the court would not consider the time necessary for such a check to constitute unduly prolonging the stop.

The Arrest Warrant and Other Criminal Process (page 56)

Legislation enacted in 2017[55] amended G.S. 15A-304 in a manner affecting the discussion in the main text of arrest warrants and criminal summonses. On page 60, the main text explains that a criminal summons should be used instead of an arrest warrant when it appears that the defendant will come to court as required without the need to arrest the defendant and set conditions of pretrial release. For a brief period of time subsequent to the publication of the main text, G.S. 15A-304(b) expressed a preference that a judicial official issue a criminal summons rather than an arrest warrant in even stronger terms than was the case when the main text was published, providing that an issuing official "shall issue a criminal summons instead of a warrant, unless the official finds that the accused should be taken into custody."[56] The amended statute provided a non-exclusive list of circumstances to be considered in determining whether the accused should be taken into custody.[57] Legislation enacted in 2018[58] repealed the amendment just described, returning the relevant portion of the statute to the form it was in when the main text was published.

The same 2017 legislation placed new restrictions on citizen-initiated criminal process, one of which was eliminated by the 2018 legislation described above. Under the statute as amended in 2017, probable cause supporting citizen-initiated criminal process could only be provided by written affidavit. This change in the law affected the discussion in the "Issuance and content" section on pages 57 and 58 of the main text, which explains that a person may present facts supporting probable cause to a magistrate by either written affidavit or oral testimony. While the 2017 amendments were in effect, the discussion in the main text continued to be accurate when the person providing facts supporting probable cause was a sworn law enforcement officer. Under the 2018 legislation, effective October 1, 2018, citizen-initiated criminal process once again may be based on oral testimony, as was the case when the main text was published.

One of the changes to G.S. 15A-304 introduced by the 2017 legislation was not affected by the 2018 legislation. The statute now provides that in cases when the person providing probable cause information is not a sworn law enforcement officer, an issuing official "shall not issue a warrant for arrest and instead shall issue a criminal summons" unless (1) there is corroborating testimony of the facts establishing probable cause from a sworn law enforcement officer or at least one disinterested witness, (2) the issuing official finds that obtaining investigation of the alleged offense by a law enforcement agency would constitute a substantial burden for the complainant, or (3) the issuing official finds substantial evidence of one or more grounds for taking the accused into custody as listed in G.S. 15A-304(b)(1).[59]

---

54. *Id.*

55. S.L. 2017-176.

56. *Id.*

57. *Id.*

58. S.L. 2018-40.

59. *Id.*

Arrest Without a Warrant or Order for Arrest (page 62)
Taking Custody of Juveniles for Delinquent Acts and Other Matters (page 66)

This section of the main text discusses the authority of law enforcement officers to take custody of juveniles under the age of 16 when there is probable cause to believe that the juvenile is delinquent and the same reasons exist to justify temporary custody as would justify a warrantless arrest of an adult. The Juvenile Justice Reinvestment Act, commonly known as the "raise the age" law, took effect for offenses committed on or after December 1, 2019, and raised the age of juvenile jurisdiction to 18 for most purposes.[60] As it relates to this section of the main text, the raise the age law amended the definition of the term *delinquent juvenile* in G.S. 7B-1501(7) to include "[a]ny juvenile who, while less than 18 years of age but at least 16 years of age, commits a crime or an infraction under State law or under an ordinance of local government, excluding all violations of the motor vehicle laws under Chapter 20 of the General Statutes, or who commits indirect contempt by a juvenile as defined in G.S. 5A-31." Thus, under the raise the age law, the discussion in the main text regarding taking temporary custody of juveniles under the age of 16 also is applicable to 16- and 17-year-olds, except when the offense at issue involves a violation of the motor vehicle laws. If someone under the age of 18 commits a new offense following his or her conviction in superior court or district court for any offense other than a misdemeanor Chapter 20 motor vehicle offense that did not involve impaired driving or commercial impaired driving, that person is no longer eligible for juvenile jurisdiction. Therefore, if a minor has one of these previous convictions, the procedures for taking a juvenile into custody do not apply. Likewise, if a youth is emancipated, he or she does not fall under juvenile jurisdiction for any offense and the procedures for taking a juvenile into custody do not apply.

Legislation enacted in 2020 altered the place of confinement for any person under 18 who is being charged as an adult.[61] Pursuant to this law, any person under 18 who is being charged as an adult and who is not released pending trial must be held in a juvenile detention facility. While the place of confinement for these minors is juvenile detention, the procedures for taking them into custody remain the adult criminal procedures.

The Arrest Procedure (page 67)
Entering Defendant's Home or Other Place of Residence without Consent or Exigent Circumstances (page 71)
Exigent Circumstances That Justify Entering Premises (page 74)

In *State v. Adams*,[62] the North Carolina Court of Appeals held that exigent circumstances supported officers entering the defendant's home to arrest him for resisting a public officer. While on routine patrol, officers observed the defendant driving a motor vehicle and developed reasonable suspicion that the defendant was driving while his license was revoked. The officers pulled into the defendant's driveway, where he had just parked, and initiated a traffic stop by activating blue lights. By the time the lights were activated, the defendant already had exited his vehicle and was walking towards the front door of his home. An officer instructed the

---

60. *See generally* S.L. 2017-57, § 16D.4, *as amended by* S.L. 2019-186. See also the following resources written by School of Government faculty member Jacquelyn Greene: JUVENILE JUSTICE REINVESTMENT ACT IMPLEMENTATION GUIDE (UNC School of Government, 2019); *Raise the Age: Modifications and Training Opportunities*, UNC SCH. OF GOV'T: N.C. CRIM. L. BLOG (Aug. 27, 2019), https://nccriminallaw.sog.unc.edu/raise-the-age-modifications-and-training-opportunities/; *Raise the Age FAQs*, UNC SCH. OF GOV'T: N.C. CRIM. L. BLOG (Oct. 22, 2019), https://nccriminallaw.sog.unc.edu/raise-the-age-faqs/; *Raise the Age Tips and Resources for Law Enforcement*, UNC SCH. OF GOV'T: N.C. CRIM. L. BLOG (Nov. 26, 2019), https://nccriminallaw.sog.unc.edu/raise-the-age-tips-and-resources-for-law-enforcement/.

61. S.L. 2020-83, effective for offenses committed, sentences imposed, and any other orders of imprisonment issued on or after August 1, 2020.

62. 250 N.C. App. 664 (2016).

defendant to stop, but he disregarded the command, entered the front door, and attempted to close the door on an officer in pursuit. The officers prevented the defendant from closing the door, entered his home, and arrested him. The court found that the defendant's failure to stop for the blue lights and his disregard of the officer's commands gave the officers probable cause to arrest him for resisting an officer; the situation became one of "hot pursuit" as the defendant hurried towards the door to his house. Citing *United States v. Santana*,[63] the court held that the officers' hot pursuit of defendant was an exigent circumstance sufficient to justify a warrantless entry and arrest of the defendant inside his home.[64] The court rejected the defendant's argument that the entry was unreasonable because there was no threat of violence, no evidence subject to destruction, and no likelihood of the defendant fleeing his home to elude detection. The court also rejected the defendant's argument that the officers' decision to engage in hot pursuit was unreasonable.

Completion of Custody of the Arrestee (page 79)
Taking Fingerprints and Photographs (page 81)

Statutory changes since the main text was written have affected the discussion in this section of fingerprinting and photographing both adults and juveniles. The most significant legislation was the Juvenile Justice Reinvestment Act (and subsequent amendments), commonly known as the "raise the age" law, which took effect for offenses committed on and after December 1, 2019. The act raised the age of juvenile jurisdiction from under 16 to under 18 years old for most purposes. The law amended the definition of the term *delinquent juvenile* in G.S. 7B-1501(7) to include "[a]ny juvenile who, while less than 18 years of age but at least 16 years of age, commits a crime or an infraction under State law or under an ordinance of local government, excluding all violations of the motor vehicle laws under Chapter 20 of the General Statutes, or who commits indirect contempt by a juvenile as defined in G.S. 5A-31."[65] Thus, the only offenses committed at ages 16 and 17 that should not be charged as juvenile offenses are motor vehicle offenses under Chapter 20 of the General Statutes.

The raise the age law also contained provisions that bar from juvenile jurisdiction any person who would otherwise fall under juvenile jurisdiction when that person commits a new offense following a previous disqualifying criminal conviction. G.S. 7B-1604(b) was amended by S.L. 2019-186 to provide that any juvenile under 18 years old must be prosecuted as an adult for any criminal offense the juvenile commits after a district or superior court conviction if (1) the juvenile has previously been transferred to and convicted in superior court or (2) the juvenile has previously been convicted in either district or superior court for a felony or misdemeanor, excluding violations of motor vehicle laws punishable as a misdemeanor or infraction unless the conviction was for impaired driving or commercial impaired driving. Any juvenile who obtains one of these convictions is not eligible for juvenile jurisdiction for any new offense that occurs after the conviction and should therefore be processed as an adult. When a juvenile is prosecuted as an adult, the fingerprinting and photographing provisions and nontestimonial identification statutes applicable to adults govern, not the nontestimonial identification juvenile statutes.[66] Remember, however, as discussed in the first full paragraph

---

63. 427 U.S. 38 (1976).

64. *Adams*, 250 N.C. App. at 671.

65. *See generally* S.L. 2017-57, § 16D.4, *as amended by* S.L. 2019-186. See also the resources from School of Government faculty member Jacquelyn Greene cited in note 60, *supra*.

66. See the first sentence of G.S. 7B-2103 ("nontestimonial identification procedures shall not be conducted on any juvenile without a court order . . . unless the juvenile has been charged as an adult or transferred to superior court for trial as an adult in which case procedures applicable to adults . . . shall apply").

on page 82 of the main text, there are limitations to fingerprinting and photographing an adult arrested for a motor vehicle offense.[67]

Because the legislative "raise the age" act revised existing law, the paragraph on page 82 of the main text beginning with "Although there is some uncertainty about what age constitutes an adult for the purpose of fingerprinting and photographing" and footnote 439 are no longer relevant and therefore should be disregarded.

Officers who are unsure of these legal provisions should consult with their agency's legal advisor or their district attorney to determine how they should handle photographing and fingerprinting.

Footnote 442 on page 83 is rewritten as follows: G.S. 7B-1604 provides in part that a juvenile who is emancipated must be prosecuted as an adult and that a juvenile must be prosecuted as an adult for any criminal offense the juvenile commits after a district or superior court conviction if (1) the juvenile has previously been transferred to and convicted in superior court or (2) the juvenile has previously been convicted in either district or superior court for a felony or misdemeanor, but a misdemeanor violation of the motor vehicle laws is not considered a conviction for this purpose unless the conviction is for an offense involving impaired driving as defined in G.S. 20-4.01(24a). A juvenile who violates Chapter 20 of the General Statutes at age 16 or 17 is prosecuted as an adult. However, remember that an arrestee charged with a motor vehicle offense, whether an adult or a juvenile prosecuted as an adult, may not be fingerprinted or photographed if the offense is a Class 2 or Class 3 misdemeanor, except for photographing the arrestee for identification purposes if the conditions set out in G.S. 15A-502(b) are satisfied.

Considering Pretrial Release Conditions (page 86)

In *State v. Mitchell*,[68] the North Carolina Court of Appeals held that judicially ordered restrictions prohibiting the defendant from contacting his romantic partner, who was the alleged victim of the defendant's assaultive conduct, were in effect while the defendant was in pretrial detention despite the fact that the restrictions were described in portions of court orders ostensibly setting the defendant's conditions of pretrial release. In reaching this holding, the court rejected the defendant's argument that he did not become subject to the restrictions until he was released from detention and, thus, that he did not violate the restrictions by contacting his romantic partner while detained. The court reasoned that the relevant court orders were in effect and prohibited the defendant's conduct regardless of the fact that he had not been released from detention.

---

67. An arrestee, whether an adult or a juvenile, who is charged with a motor vehicle offense may not be fingerprinted or photographed if the offense is a Class 2 or Class 3 misdemeanor, with a limited exception for photographing the arrestee for identification purposes if the conditions set out in G.S. 15A-502(b) are satisfied.

68. 259 N.C. App. 866 (2018).

Chapter 2 Appendix: Case Summaries

Arrests, Investigative Stops, and Related Issues (page 97)

The Authority to Make an Investigative Stop: Reasonable Suspicion (page 99)
Determination of Reasonable Suspicion (page 99)
Generally (page 99)
NORTH CAROLINA SUPREME COURT (page 102)

State v. Ellis, 374 N.C. 340 (2020), *rev'g* ___ N.C. App. ___, 832 S.E.2d 750 (2019). The court ruled that reasonable suspicion of criminal activity (disorderly conduct) did not exist to justify an officer's stop of a vehicle when the defendant gestured with his middle finger from the vehicle's passenger side.

State v. Nicholson, 371 N.C. 284, 286 (2018) (footnote omitted). On appeal from the decision of a divided panel of the court of appeals, 255 N.C. App. 665 (2017), the state supreme court reversed, holding that an officer's decision to briefly detain the defendant for questioning was supported by reasonable suspicion of criminal activity. While on patrol at 4 a.m., Lieutenant Marotz noticed a car parked in a turn lane of the street, with its headlights on but no turn signal blinking. Marotz saw two men inside the vehicle, one in the driver's seat and the other—later identified as the defendant—in the seat directly behind the driver. The windows were down despite rain and low temperatures. As Marotz pulled alongside the vehicle, he saw the defendant pull down a hood or toboggan-style mask with holes for the eyes, but then push the item back up when he saw the officer. Marotz asked the two whether everything was okay and they responded that it was. The driver said that the man in the back was his brother and they had been arguing. The driver said the argument was over and everything was okay. Sensing that something was not right, the officer again asked if they were okay, and they nodded that they were. Then the driver moved his hand near his neck, "scratching or doing something with his hand." Still feeling that something was amiss, Marotz drove to a nearby gas station to observe the situation. After the car remained immobile in the turn lane for another half minute, Marotz got out of his vehicle and started on foot towards the car. The defendant stepped out of the vehicle and the driver began to edge the car forward. Marotz asked the driver what he was doing, and the driver said he was late and had to get to work. The officer again asked whether everything was okay, and the men said that everything was fine. However, although the driver responded "yes" to the officer's question, he shook his head "no." This prompted the officer to further question the defendant. The driver insisted he just had to get to work and the officer told him to go. After the driver left, the defendant asked the officer if he could walk to a nearby store. The officer responded, "[H]ang tight for me just a second . . . you don't have any weapons on you, do you?" The defendant said he had a knife, but a frisk by a backup officer did not reveal a weapon. After additional questioning the officers learned the defendant's identity and told him he was free to go. Later that day the driver reported to the police that the defendant was not his brother and had been robbing him when Marotz pulled up. The defendant held a knife to the driver's throat and demanded money. Officers later found a steak knife in the back seat of the vehicle. The defendant was charged with armed robbery and moved to suppress the evidence obtained as a result of his seizure by Marotz. The parties agreed that the defendant was seized when Marotz told him to "hang tight." The court found that the circumstances established a reasonable, articulable suspicion that criminal activity was afoot. Although the facts might not establish reasonable suspicion when viewed in isolation, when considered in their totality they could lead a reasonable officer to suspect that he had just happened upon a robbery in progress. The court also found that the court of appeals placed undue weight on Marotz's subjective interpretation of the facts (the officer's testimony suggested that he did not believe he had reasonable suspicion of criminal activity), rather than focusing on how an objective, reasonable officer would have viewed them. The court noted that an action is reasonable under the Fourth Amendment, regardless of the officer's state of mind, if the circumstances viewed objectively justify the action. Here they did.

State v. Goins, 370 N.C. 157 (2017). For the reasons stated in the dissenting opinion below, the state supreme court reversed the decision of the court of appeals in *State v. Goins*, 248 N.C. App. 265 (2016). In that case, the court of appeals held, over a dissent, that a stop of the defendant's vehicle was not supported by reasonable suspicion. Just after midnight, officers were on patrol near an apartment complex that they knew as an area of high crime and drug activity. The officers observed a car, a Hyundai Elantra, enter the apartment complex parking lot and drive towards a man standing in front of one of the apartment buildings. The man looked directly at their patrol vehicle and then made a loud "warning noise" directed at the Elantra. Immediately thereafter, the Elantra accelerated and quickly exited the apartment complex, an action the trial court characterized as unprovoked fleeing from the officers. The dissenting judge in the court of appeals concluded, under a totality of the circumstances analysis, that the officers had reasonable suspicion to justify an investigatory stop of the Elantra based on the vehicle's presence in a high-crime area and its apparent flight from the officers.

NORTH CAROLINA COURT OF APPEALS (page 106)

State v. Holley, ___ N.C. App. ___, 833 S.E.2d 63 (2019). The court ruled that some of the evidence at a suppression hearing did not support the trial court's findings of fact in its denial of the defendant's suppression motion. The court ruled, relying on *State v. White*, 214 N.C. App. 471 (2011), and other cases, that the anonymous report of a drug deal on a specific street corner involving two black males, an officer's later seeing the defendant and another black male there, and the defendant's walking away from the officer did not provide reasonable suspicion to stop or probable cause to arrest for obstructing the officer.

State v. Horton, 264 N.C. App. 711 (2019). The court ruled that an officer's investigative stop of a vehicle was not supported by reasonable suspicion to make the stop. An anonymous tip concerning a suspicious white male in a gold or silver vehicle in a certain parking lot reported no crime and was only partially corroborated. Although there was a silver car in that parking lot, there was no white male in the lot or in the vehicle (the defendant was a black male). In addition, the tip merely described the individual as "suspicious" without any indication about why. No information existed about who the tipster was and what made the tipster reliable. As a result, there was nothing inherent in the tip itself to allow a court to consider it reliable and provide reasonable suspicion. The officer's observations independent of the tip also did not provide reasonable suspicion for the stop. The trial court's findings of fact concerning the officer's knowledge about criminal activity at the location referred to the area in general and were without particularized facts. The officer did not say how he was familiar with the area, how he knew that there had been break-ins, or how much vandalism or other crimes had occurred there. The trial court's findings found that there was no specific time frame given for when the previous break-ins had occurred.

State v. Malachi, 264 N.C. App. 233, 238 (2019). The court ruled that the trial court did not err by allowing evidence of a handgun an officer removed from the defendant's waistband during a lawful frisk that occurred after a lawful stop. Police received an anonymous 911 call stating that an African-American male wearing a red shirt and black pants had just placed a handgun in the waistband of his pants while at a specified gas station. Officer Clark responded to the scene and saw six to eight people in the parking lot, including a person who matched the description in the 911 call, later identified as the defendant. As Clark got out of his car, the defendant looked directly at him, "bladed" away, and started to walk away. Clark and a second officer grabbed the defendant. After Clark placed the defendant in handcuffs and told him that he was not under arrest, the second officer frisked the defendant and found a revolver in his waistband. The court ruled that the trial court did not err by denying the motion to suppress. Although the anonymous tip was insufficient by itself to provide reasonable suspicion for the stop, there was additional evidence. As Clark left his car, the defendant turned his body in such a way as to prevent the officer from seeing a weapon. The officer testified that the type of turn the defendant executed was known as "blading," which is "[w]hen you have a gun on your hip you tend to blade it away from an individual." In addition, the defendant began to move away. And, as the officers approached the defendant, the defendant did not inform them that he was lawfully armed. Under the totality of the circumstances, these facts support reasonable suspicion.

The court also ruled that the frisk was proper because there was reasonable suspicion to believe that the defendant was armed and dangerous.

State v. Augustin, 264 N.C. App. 81, 84 (2019). While patrolling a high-crime area, an officer saw the defendant and Ariel Peterson walking on a sidewalk. Aware of multiple recent crimes in the area, the officer stopped his car and approached the men. The officer had prior interactions with the defendant and knew he lived some distance away. The officer asked the men for their names. Peterson initially gave a false name; the defendant did not. The officer asked them where they were coming from and where they were going. Both gave vague answers; they claimed to have been at Peterson's girlfriend's house and said they were walking back to the defendant's home, but they were unable or unwilling to say where the girlfriend lived. When the defendant asked the officer for a ride to his house, the officer agreed and the three walked to the patrol car. The officer informed the two that police procedure required him to search them before entering the car. As the officer began to frisk Peterson, Peterson ran away. The officer turned to the defendant, who had begun stepping away. Believing the defendant was about to run away, the officer grabbed the defendant's shoulders, placed the defendant on the ground, and handcuffed him. As the officer helped the defendant up, he saw that a gun had fallen out of the defendant's waistband.

The court rejected the defendant's argument that he was unlawfully seized when the officer discovered the gun. Agreeing with the defendant that exercising a constitutional right to leave a consensual encounter should not be used against a defendant "to tip the scale towards reasonable suspicion," the court noted that the manner in which a defendant exercises this right "could, in some cases, be used to tip the scale." However, the court found that it need not determine whether it was appropriate for the trial court to consider the fact that the defendant was backing away in its reasonable suspicion calculus. Rather, the trial court's findings regarding the men's behavior before the defendant backed away from the officer were sufficient to support reasonable suspicion. The defendant was in an area where a "spree of crime" had occurred; Peterson lied about his name; both men gave the officer vague answers about where they were coming from; and Peterson ran away while being searched. This evidence supports the trial court's conclusion that the officer had reasonable suspicion to seize the defendant.

State v. Baskins, 260 N.C. App. 589, 606 (2018). In a case in which the court determined that the defendant received ineffective assistance of appellate counsel, the court considered whether there was reasonable suspicion for a stop of the defendant's vehicle and found there was none. The trial court's conclusion that the stopping officers had reasonable suspicion to stop the vehicle was based solely on the following facts: officers saw the defendant and a woman exit a China Bus carrying small bags at the "same bus stop that a lot of heroin is being transported from New York to the Greensboro area." While waiting for his ride at an adjacent gas station, the defendant briefly looked towards an officer's unmarked vehicle and "shooed" that vehicle away, at which point the defendant's ride pulled into the parking lot. These facts do not support a finding of reasonable suspicion, particularly when the defendant was entirely unknown to the officers.

State v. Sutton, 259 N.C. App. 891, 893 (2018). In this drug trafficking case, the court held that the fact that the defendant's truck crossed over a double yellow line justified a stop. The stopping officer saw the defendant's vehicle cross the center line of the road by about 1 inch. The court stated:

> [T]here is a "bright line" rule in some traffic stop cases. Here, the bright line is a double yellow line down the center of the road. Where a vehicle actually crosses over the double yellow lines in the center of a road, even once, and even without endangering any other drivers, the driver has committed a

traffic violation of N.C. Gen. Stat. § 20-146 (2017). This is a "readily observable" traffic violation and the officer may stop the driver without violating his constitutional rights.

State v. Walker, 255 N.C. App. 828 (2017). The court ruled that reasonable suspicion did not exist to support a stop. At approximately 5 p.m., dispatch notified a trooper on routine patrol that an informant-driver reported that another driver was driving while intoxicated. The informant reported that the driver was driving from the Hubert area towards Jacksonville, traveling about 80 to 100 m.p.h. while drinking a beer. He also claimed that the driver was driving "very erratically" and almost ran him off the road "a few times." While the trooper was responding to the dispatch, the informant flagged him down and said that the vehicle in question had just passed through the intersection on U.S. 258, heading towards Richlands. The trooper headed in that direction and stopped the defendant's vehicle within 1/10 of a mile of the intersection. The defendant was arrested and charged with DWI and careless and reckless driving. The defendant unsuccessfully moved to suppress evidence obtained by the stop in district court and appealed to superior court. After a hearing, the superior court granted the motion to suppress. The court of appeals found that the tip did not have sufficient indicia of reliability to provide reasonable suspicion for the stop. Although the informant was not anonymous, the informant was unable to specifically point out the defendant's vehicle to the trooper because the vehicle was out of sight. The trooper did not observe the vehicle being driven in a suspicious or erratic fashion. Additionally, it is unknown whether the trooper had the vehicle's license plate number before or after the stop and whether the trooper had any vehicle description besides a "gray Ford passenger vehicle." The court distinguished prior case law involving tips that provided enough information so that there was no doubt as to which particular vehicle was being reported. Here, the informant's ambiguous description did not specify a particular vehicle. Additionally, no other circumstances enabled the trooper to further corroborate the tip; the trooper did not witness the vehicle behaving as described by the informant.

State v. Sauls, 255 N.C. App. 684 (2017). The court ruled that reasonable suspicion supported an officer's traffic stop. At the time of the stop it was very late at night, the defendant's vehicle was idling in front of a closed business, the business and surrounding properties had experienced several break-ins, and the defendant pulled away when the officer approached the car. Considered together, these facts provided an objective justification for stopping the defendant.

State v. Evans, 251 N.C. App. 610 (2017). The court ruled that reasonable suspicion supported the stop at issue. An officer patrolling a "known drug corridor" at 4 a.m. observed the defendant's car stopped in the lane of traffic. An unidentified pedestrian approached the defendant's car and leaned in the window. The officer found these actions to be indicative of a drug transaction and thus conducted the stop.

State v. Watson, 250 N.C. App. 455 (2016). In this drug case, the trial court erred by denying the defendant's motion to suppress drug evidence seized after a traffic stop where the stopping officer had no reasonable suspicion to stop the defendant's vehicle. Officers received a tip from a confidential informant regarding "suspicious" packages that the defendant had received from a local UPS store. The informant was an employee of the UPS store trained to detect narcotics; the informant had successfully notified the police about packages later found to contain illegal drugs, and these tips were used to secure a number of felony drug convictions. With respect to the incident in question, the informant advised the police that a man, later identified as the defendant, had arrived at the UPS store in a truck and retrieved packages with a Utah return address when in fact the packages had been sent from Arizona. After receiving this tip, the police arrived at the store, observed the defendant driving away, and initiated a traffic stop. During the stop they conducted a canine sniff, which led to the discovery of drugs inside the packages. Holding that the motion to suppress should have been granted, the court noted that there is nothing illegal about receiving a package with a return address that differs from the actual shipping address; in fact, there are a number of innocent explanations for why this could have occurred. Although innocent factors, when considered together, may give rise to reasonable suspicion, the court noted that it was unable to find any case where reasonable suspicion was based solely on a suspicious return address. Here, the trial court made no finding that the informant or the police had any prior experience with the defendant; that the origination city was known as a drug-source locale; nor that the packages were sealed suspiciously, had a suspicious weight based on their size, had handwritten labels, or had a suspicious odor.

DWI Stops (page 120)
NORTH CAROLINA SUPREME COURT (page 120)

State v. Carver, 373 N.C. 453 (2020). The supreme court, per curiam and without an opinion, affirmed the ruling of the court of appeals, ___ N.C. App. ___, 828 S.E.2d 195 (2019), that reasonable suspicion did not support a warrantless traffic stop based on an anonymous tip.

A sheriff's deputy received a dispatch call, originating from an anonymous tipster, just before 11 p.m. The deputy was advised about a vehicle in a ditch on a specified road, possibly with a "drunk driver, someone intoxicated" and that "a truck was attempting—getting ready to pull them out." The tip provided no description of the car, truck, or driver, nor was there information regarding the caller or when the call was received. When the deputy arrived at the scene about ten minutes later, he noticed a white Cadillac at an angle partially in someone's driveway. The vehicle had mud on the driver's side, and the deputy opined from gouges in the road that it was the vehicle that had run off the road. However, he continued driving and saw a truck travelling away from his location. He estimated that the truck was travelling approximately 15 to 20 m.p.h. below the posted 55 m.p.h. speed limit. He testified that the truck was the only one on the highway and that it was big enough to pull the car out. He did not see any chains, straps, or other devices that would indicate it had just pulled the vehicle out of the ditch. He initiated a traffic stop. His sole reason for doing so was "due to what was called out from communications." The truck was driven by Griekspoor, and the defendant was in the passenger seat.

After the deputy stopped the truck, he explained to the driver that there was a report of a truck attempting to pull a vehicle out of a ditch. The driver reported that he had pulled the defendant's car out of the ditch and was giving him a ride home. The deputy's supervisor arrived and went to talk with the defendant. The defendant was given a Breathalyzer and eventually charged with impaired driving. At trial he unsuccessfully moved to suppress evidence, was convicted, and appealed.

The court found that the stop was improper because it was not supported by reasonable suspicion. As the State conceded, the anonymous tip likely failed to provide sufficient reliability to support the stop. It provided no description of either the car or the truck or how many people were involved, and there was no indication when the call came in or when the anonymous tipster saw the car in the ditch with the truck attempting to pull it out. The State argued, however, that because nearly every aspect of the tip was corroborated by the officer, there was reasonable suspicion for the stop. The court disagreed. When the deputy passed the Cadillac and came up behind the truck, he saw no equipment to indicate the truck had pulled, or was able to pull, a car out of the ditch and could not see how many people were in the truck. The deputy testified that it was not operating in violation of the law. "He believed it was a suspicious vehicle merely because of the fact it was on the highway." The details in the anonymous tip were insufficient to establish identifying characteristics, let alone allow the deputy to corroborate the details. The tipster merely indicated that a car was in a ditch, someone was present who may be intoxicated, and a truck was preparing to pull the vehicle out of the ditch. There was no description of the car, the truck, or any individuals who may have been involved. After the deputy passed the scene and the Cadillac, he noticed a truck driving under the posted speed limit. He provided no testimony to show that the truck was engaging in unsafe, reckless, or illegal driving. He was unable to ascertain if it contained a passenger. The court stated that at best there was a tip with no indicia of reliability, no corroboration, and conduct falling within the broad range of what can be described as normal driving behavior. Under the totality of the circumstances, the deputy lacked reasonable suspicion to conduct a warrantless stop of the truck.

NORTH CAROLINA COURT OF APPEALS (page 122)

State v. Neal, ___ N.C. App. ___, ___, 833 S.E.2d 367, 376 (2019). An anonymous person contacted law enforcement to report that a small green vehicle with license plate RCW-042 was in a specific area, had run several vehicles off the road, had struck a vehicle, and was attempting to leave the scene. Deputies went to the area and immediately stopped a vehicle matching the description given by the caller. The defendant was driving the vehicle. She was unsteady on her feet and appeared to be severely impaired. A trooper arrived and administered Standardized Field Sobriety Tests, which the trooper terminated because the defendant could not complete them safely. A subsequent blood test revealed multiple drugs in the defendant's system. The defendant was convicted of impaired driving.

The defendant argued that the stop was not supported by reasonable suspicion because it was based on an anonymous tip that was not corroborated by any observation of bad driving. The court disagreed, noting some tension between prior North Carolina case law emphasizing the need to corroborate anonymous tips and *Navarette v. California*, 572 U.S. 393 (2014), which found reasonable suspicion of impaired driving based on an anonymous caller's report that a vehicle had nearly run the caller off the road. The court stated that it "need not resolve the apparent tension between our previous case law and *Navarette*" because the tip in this case involved a very timely and specific report of multiple driving incidents and thus was sufficiently reliable to support reasonable suspicion.

State v. Cabbagestalk, ___ N.C. App. ___, ___, ___, 830 S.E.2d 5, 10, 11 (2019). In this driving while impaired case, an officer observed the defendant sitting on a porch and drinking a tall beer at approximately 9:00 p.m. The defendant was known to the officer as someone he had previously stopped for driving while license revoked and an open container offense. Around 11:00 p.m., the officer encountered the defendant at a gas station, where she paid for another beer and returned to her car. The officer did not observe any signs of impairment while observing her at the store and did not speak to her. When the defendant drove away from the store, the officer followed her and saw her driving "normally"—she did not speed or drive too slow, she did not weave or swerve, she did not drink the beer, and otherwise conformed to all rules of the road. After two or three blocks, the officer stopped the car. He testified that the stop was based on having seen her drinking beer earlier in the evening, purchasing more beer at the store later, and then driving away. The court noted that a traffic violation is not always necessary for reasonable suspicion to stop (collecting sample cases), but observed that "when the basis for an officer's suspicion connects only tenuously with the criminal behavior suspected, if at all, courts have not found the requisite reasonable suspicion." Here, the officer did not have information that the defendant was impaired and did not observe any traffic violations. The court also rejected the State's argument that the defendant's past criminal history for driving while license revoked and open container supplemented the officer's suspicions: "Prior charges alone, however, do not provide the requisite reasonable suspicion and these particular priors are too attenuated from the facts of the current controversy to aid the State's argument." The court ruled that the trial court's finding of reasonable suspicion was erroneous.

State v. Mangum, 250 N.C. App. 714 (2016). The court ruled that a vehicle stop was supported by reasonable suspicion. An officer received an anonymous report that a drunk driver was operating a black, four-door Hyundai headed north on Highland Capital Boulevard. The officer located the vehicle as reported and observed that the defendant drove roughly 15 m.p.h. below the 35 m.p.h. speed limit; that the defendant stopped at an intersection without a stop sign or traffic signal for "longer than usual"; that the defendant stopped at a railroad crossing and remained motionless for fifteen to twenty seconds, although no train was coming and there was no signal to stop; and that after the officer activated his blue lights, the defendant continued driving for approximately two minutes, eventually stopping in the middle of the road, and in a portion of the road with no bank or curb, having passed several safe places to pull over.

Non-DWI Traffic Stops (page 125)

UNITED STATES SUPREME COURT (page 125)

Kansas v. Glover, 589 U.S. ___, 140 S. Ct. 1183 (2020). A Kansas deputy sheriff ran a license plate check on a pickup truck and learned that the truck belonged to defendant Glover and that Glover's driver's license had been revoked. The deputy pulled the truck over because he assumed that Glover was driving. Glover was in fact driving and was charged with driving as a habitual violator. The Court ruled that when the registered owner of a vehicle has a revoked driver's license and an officer lacks information negating an inference that the owner is the driver of the vehicle, the stop is reasonable under the Fourth Amendment. The Court gave as an example of when the inference would be negated a situation where an officer knows that the owner of a vehicle is in his mid-sixties but the driver is in her mid-twenties.

NORTH CAROLINA SUPREME COURT (page 126)

State v. Johnson, 370 N.C. 32, 37, 38 (2017). The supreme court reversed the ruling of the court of appeals, 246 N.C. App. 671 (2016), a case summarized on page 129 of the main text, which had held that because a police officer lacked reasonable suspicion for a traffic stop in this DWI case, the trial court erred by denying the defendant's motion to suppress evidence obtained as a result of the stop. The defendant was stopped at a red light on a snowy evening. When the light turned green, the officer saw the defendant's truck abruptly accelerate, turn sharply left, and fishtail. The officer pulled the defendant over for driving at an unsafe speed given the road conditions. The state supreme court held that the officer had reasonable suspicion to stop the defendant's vehicle. It noted that G.S. 20-141(a) provides that "[n]o person shall drive a vehicle on a highway or in a public vehicular area at a speed greater than is reasonable and prudent under the conditions then existing." The court concluded:

> All of these facts show that it was reasonable for [the] Officer . . . to believe that defendant's truck had fishtailed, and that defendant had lost control of his truck, because of defendant's abrupt acceleration while turning in the snow. It is common knowledge that drivers must drive more slowly when it is snowing, because it is easier to lose control of a vehicle on snowy roads than on clear ones. And any time that a driver loses control of his vehicle, he is in danger of damaging that vehicle or other vehicles, and of injuring himself or others. So, under the totality of these circumstances, it was reasonable for [the] Officer . . . to believe that defendant had violated [G.S.] 20-141(a) by driving too quickly given the conditions of the road.

The court further noted that no actual traffic violation need have occurred for a stop to be initiated. It clarified: "To meet the reasonable suspicion standard, it is enough for the officer to *reasonably believe* that a driver has violated the law."

NORTH CAROLINA COURT OF APPEALS (page 129)

State v. Wiles, ___ N.C. App. ___, 841 S.E.2d 321 (2020). The court ruled that an officer had reasonable suspicion to conduct a traffic stop due to his reasonable but mistaken belief that a passenger was not wearing a seatbelt. The officer's mistake—failing to see a gray seatbelt atop a gray shirt—was one a reasonable officer could make.

State v. Jones, 258 N.C. App. 643 (2018). An officer's observation of a single instance of a vehicle crossing the double yellow centerline in violation of state motor vehicle law provided reasonable suspicion to support the traffic stop. While traveling southbound on Highway 32, N.C. Highway Patrol Trooper Myers was notified by dispatch that a caller had reported a black Chevrolet truck traveling northbound on Highway 32 at a careless, reckless, and high speed. Myers then saw a black Chevrolet truck traveling northbound cross the center double yellow line. Myers initiated a traffic stop, which resulted in impaired-driving charges. The defendant argued that the stop was not supported by reasonable suspicion because Myers did not corroborate the caller's information. The court rejected this argument, noting that Myers's own observation of the vehicle driving left of center provided reasonable suspicion for the stop. Under G.S. 20-150(d), crossing a double yellow centerline constitutes a traffic violation. Citing prior case law, the court stated that an officer's observation of such a violation is sufficient to constitute reasonable suspicion for a traffic stop.

State v. Eldridge, 249 N.C. App. 493, 499, 500 (2016). The court ruled that the trial court erred by denying the defendant's motion to suppress evidence obtained as a result of a stop where the stop was based on an officer's mistake of law that was not objectively reasonable. An officer stopped a vehicle registered in Tennessee for driving without an exterior mirror on the driver's side of the vehicle. The officer was not aware that the relevant statute—G.S. 20-126(b)—does not apply to vehicles registered out of state. A subsequent consent search led to the discovery of controlled substances and drug charges. On appeal, the State conceded, and the court concluded, following *Heien v. North Carolina*, 574 U.S. 54 (2014), that the officer's mistake of law was not reasonable. Looking for guidance in other jurisdictions that have interpreted *Heien*, the court noted that cases from other jurisdictions "establish that in order for an officer's mistake of law while enforcing a statute to be objectively reasonable, the statute at issue must be ambiguous." "Moreover," the court noted, "some courts applying *Heien* have further required that there be an absence of settled case law interpreting the statute at issue in order for the officer's mistake of law to be deemed objectively reasonable." The court concluded that the statute at issue was clear and unambiguous; as a result, "a reasonable officer reading this statute would understand the requirement that a vehicle be equipped with a driver's side exterior mirror does not apply to vehicles that—like Defendant's vehicle—are registered in another state."

Special Aspects of Stopping Authority (page 137)
Length of Time Allowed for an Investigative Stop (page 137)
NORTH CAROLINA SUPREME COURT (page 139)

State v. Reed, 373 N.C. 498, 502, 511 (2020). The court ruled, distinguishing its prior ruling in *State v. Bullock*, 370 N.C. 256 (2017), discussed below, that a state trooper (Lamm) who stopped a rental car that was speeding prolonged the stop without having the defendant's voluntary consent or reasonable suspicion of criminal activity. There were two people in the car, the male defendant-driver and a female passenger who rented the vehicle. Lamm had the defendant sit in his patrol car while he checked on the status of the rental car and asked some questions about his travel plans. After about twenty minutes and upon confirming that the rental car matter was in order, Lamm returned all paperwork to the defendant and told the defendant that the stop had ended but then said, "I'm going to ask you a few more questions if it is okay with you." Lamm asked the defendant for consent to search the vehicle, to which he replied, "you could break the car down" but then further explained that the trooper should seek consent from the female passenger because she had rented the car. Lamm told the defendant to "sit tight" in the patrol car as he went to confer with her in the rental car. A backup trooper (Ellerbe), who had arrived since the stop had occurred, stationed himself outside the door of Lamm's patrol car while the defendant remained in the passenger seat with the door closed. Lamm obtained consent to search from the female passenger, and cocaine was discovered in the rental car. The court found that trooper Lamm's conduct was authorized by *Bullock* up to his unequivocal statement to the defendant that the traffic stop had been concluded. However, the traffic stop after this point became unlawful under *Rodriguez v. United States,* 575 U.S. 348 (2015), because the trooper "prolonged it beyond the time reasonably required to complete its mission." And the defendant was unconstitutionally detained beyond the announced end of the traffic stop because reasonable suspicion did not exist to justify the defendant's further detention (see the court's discussion of the facts involving the reasonable suspicion issue). The court also rejected the State's argument that the defendant consented to prolonging the traffic stop, relying in significant part on Trooper Lamm's telling the defendant to "sit tight" in the trooper's vehicle and Trooper Ellerbe's standing by the door where the defendant was seated.

State v. Downey, 370 N.C. 507 (2018). The state supreme court, per curiam and without an opinion, affirmed a ruling of the court of appeals, 251 N.C. App. 829 (2017), upholding an order denying the defendant's motion to suppress evidence obtained from a traffic stop. The court of appeals held that reasonable suspicion supported extension of the stop. After an officer stopped the defendant for a traffic violation, he approached the vehicle and asked to see the defendant's driver's license and registration. As the defendant complied, the officer noticed that his hands were shaking, his breathing was rapid, and he failed to make eye contact. He also noticed a prepaid cell phone inside the vehicle and a Black Ice air freshener. The officer had learned during drug interdiction training that Black Ice freshener is frequently used by drug traffickers because of its strong scent and that prepaid cell phones are commonly used in drug trafficking. The officer determined that the car was not registered to the defendant, and he knew from his training that third-party vehicles are often used by drug traffickers. In response to questioning about why the defendant was in the area, the defendant provided vague answers. When the officer asked the defendant about his criminal history, the defendant responded that he had served time for breaking and entering and that he had a cocaine-related drug conviction. After issuing the defendant a warning ticket for the traffic violation and returning his documentation, the officer continued to question the defendant and asked for consent to search the vehicle. The defendant declined. He also declined consent to a canine sniff. The officer then called for a canine unit, which arrived fourteen minutes after the initial stop ended. An alert led to a search of the vehicle and the discovery of contraband. The court of appeals rejected the defendant's argument that the officer lacked reasonable suspicion to extend the traffic stop, noting that before and during the time in which the officer prepared the warning citation, he observed the defendant's nervous behavior, he noted use of a particular brand of powerful air freshener favored by drug traffickers, he noticed the defendant's prepaid cell phone, he learned that the defendant's car was registered to someone else and that the defendant had a prior conviction for a drug offense, and the defendant provided only vague and suspicious answers to the officer's questions about why he was in the area. These circumstances, the court of appeals held, constituted reasonable suspicion to extend the duration of the stop.

State v. Bullock, 370 N.C. 256, 263 (2017). On an appeal from a divided panel of the court of appeals, 247 N.C. App. 412 (2016), the court reversed, concluding that the stop at issue, which was initiated based on traffic violations and where heroin ultimately was discovered, was not unduly prolonged under *Rodriguez v. United States*, 575 U.S. 348 (2015). The trial court denied the defendant's motion to suppress evidence obtained as a result of the stop and the court of appeals reversed, concluding that the stop had been unduly prolonged. During the stop, the defendant's hand trembled as he provided his license to the stopping officer. Although the car was a rental vehicle, the defendant was not listed as a driver on the rental agreement. The officer noticed that the defendant had two cell phones, a fact he associated, based on experience, with transporting drugs. The defendant was stopped on I-85, a major drug trafficking thoroughfare. When the officer asked the defendant where he was going, the defendant said he was going to his girlfriend's house on Century Oaks Drive and that he had missed his exit. The officer knew, however, that the defendant was well past the exit for that location, having passed three exits that would have taken him there. The defendant said he had recently moved to North Carolina. The officer asked the defendant to step out of the vehicle and sit in the patrol car, telling him that he would receive a warning, not a ticket. At this point the officer frisked the defendant, finding $372 in cash. The defendant sat in the patrol car while the officer ran the defendant's information through law enforcement databases, and the two continued to talk. The defendant gave contradictory statements about his girlfriend. Although the defendant made eye contact with the officer when answering certain questions, he looked away when asked about his girlfriend and where he was traveling. The database checks revealed that the defendant was issued a driver's license in 2000 and that he had a criminal history in North Carolina starting in 2001, facts contradicting his earlier claim to have just moved to the state. The officer asked the defendant for permission to search the vehicle. The defendant agreed to let the officer search the vehicle but declined to allow a search of a bag and two hoodies. When the officer found the bag and hoodies in the trunk, the defendant quickly objected that the bag was not his, contradicting an earlier statement, and said he did not want it searched. The officer put the bag on the ground and a police dog alerted to it. Officers opened the bag and found a large amount of heroin. The defendant did not challenge the validity of the initial stop. The court began by noting that during a lawful stop, an officer can ask the driver to exit the vehicle. Next, it held that the frisk was lawful for two reasons. First, frisking the defendant before putting him in the patrol car enhanced officer safety. And second, where, as here, the frisk lasted only eight to nine seconds, it did not measurably prolong the stop so as to require reasonable suspicion. The court went on to find that asking the defendant to sit in the patrol car did not unlawfully extend the stop. The officer was required to check three databases before the stop could be finished, and it was not prolonged by having the defendant in the patrol car while this was done. This action took a few minutes to complete and while it was being done, the officer was free to talk with the defendant "at least up until the moment that all three database checks had been completed." The court went on to conclude that the conversation the two had while the database checks were running provided reasonable suspicion to prolong the stop. It noted that I-85 is a major drug trafficking corridor, the defendant was nervous and had two cell phones, the rental car was in someone else's name, the defendant gave an illogical account of where he was going, and cash was discovered during the frisk. All of these facts provided reasonable suspicion of drug activity that justified prolonging the stop shortly after the defendant entered the patrol car. There, as he continued his conversation with the officer, he gave inconsistent statements about his girlfriend and the database check revealed that he had not been truthful about a recent move to North Carolina. This, combined with the defendant's broken eye contact, allowed the officer to extend the stop for purposes of the dog sniff.

NORTH CAROLINA COURT OF APPEALS (page 140)

State v. Jones, 264 N.C. App. 225, 231 (2019). The court ruled that the trial court did not err by denying the defendant's motion to suppress that alleged that officers improperly extended a traffic stop. Officers initiated a traffic stop of the vehicle for a passenger seatbelt violation. The defendant was in the passenger seat. That seat was leaned very far back while the defendant was leaning forward with his head near his knees in an awkward position. The defendant's hands were around his waist, not visible to the officer. The officer believed that based on the defendant's position he was possibly hiding a gun. When the officer introduced himself, the defendant glanced up, looked around the front area of the vehicle, but did not change position. The officer testified that the defendant's behavior was not typical. The defendant was unable to produce an identity document, but he stated that he was not going to lie about his identity. The officer testified that this statement was a sign of deception. The officer asked the defendant to exit the vehicle. When the defendant exited, he turned and pressed against the vehicle while keeping both hands around his waist. The defendant denied having any weapons and consented to a search of his person. A large wad of paper towels later fell from the defendant's pants. More than 56 grams of cocaine was in the paper towels and additional contraband was found inside the vehicle. On appeal, the defendant argued that the officer lacked reasonable suspicion to extend the traffic stop. The court disagreed, holding that the officer's conduct did not prolong the stop beyond the time reasonably required to complete its mission. When the defendant was unable to provide identification, the officer "attempted to more efficiently conduct the requisite database checks" and complete the mission of the stop by asking the defendant to exit the vehicle. Because the officer's conduct did not extend the traffic stop, no additional showing of reasonable suspicion was required.

State v. Cole, 262 N.C. App. 466 (2018). The court ruled that the trial court in a DWI case properly denied the defendant's motion to suppress evidence discovered after a roadside breath test. Specifically, the defendant asserted that the results of roadside sobriety tests and an Intoxilyzer test should be suppressed as fruit of the poisonous tree of an illegal search and seizure caused by an unlawfully compelled roadside breath test. An officer observed the defendant leave a bar after midnight and swerve several times within his driving lane. After the initial traffic stop for an observed G.S. Chapter 20 violation—the legality of which the defendant did not challenge—the officer smelled a strong odor of alcohol, the defendant presented his debit card when asked for his driver's license, and the defendant initially denied but later admitted drinking alcohol. These facts were sufficient to establish reasonable suspicion to justify prolonging the initial stop to investigate the defendant's potential impairment, including administering the roadside sobriety tests. These findings, in conjunction with findings concerning the defendant's performance on the roadside sobriety tests, supported a conclusion that the officer had probable cause to arrest the defendant for DWI, justifying the later Intoxilyzer test. Therefore, the trial court had properly refused to suppress the results of the roadside sobriety tests and the Intoxilyzer test.

State v. Sutton, 259 N.C. App. 891 (2018). The court ruled that after a proper traffic stop, an officer had reasonable suspicion to extend the stop for six or seven minutes for a dog sniff. The officer was patrolling a road because of complaints about drug activity and had been advised by the State Bureau of Investigation to be on the lookout for the defendant based upon reports that he was bringing large quantities of methamphetamine to a supplier who lived off of the road. After the officer stopped the defendant's vehicle for an observed traffic violation, he identified the defendant as the person noted in the lookout warning. The defendant was confused, spoke so quickly that he was hard to understand, and began to stutter and mumble. The defendant did not make eye contact with the officer and his nervousness was "much more extreme" than a typical stopped driver. His eyes were bloodshot and glassy and the skin under his eyes was ashy. Based on his training and experience, the officer believed the defendant's behavior and appearance were consistent with methamphetamine use. The defendant told the officer he was going to "Rabbit's" house. The officer knew that "Rabbit" was involved with methamphetamine and lived nearby. When the defendant exited his car, he put his hand on the car for stability. These facts alone could have given the officer reasonable suspicion. But additionally, a woman the officer knew who had previously given drug information to law enforcement approached and told the officer that she had talked to Rabbit and that the defendant had "dope in the vehicle." These facts were more than sufficient to give the officer a reasonable suspicion that the defendant had drugs in his vehicle and justify extension of the stop for a dog sniff.

State v. Cox, 259 N.C. App. 650 (2018). The court ruled that the traffic stop at issue was not unduly extended. The defendant, a passenger in the stopped vehicle, argued that officers extended, without reasonable suspicion, the traffic stop after issuing the driver a warning citation. The stopping officer had extensive training in drug interdiction, including the detection of behaviors by individuals tending to indicate the use, transportation, and other activity associated with controlled substances, and had investigated more than 100 drug cases. The officer observed a sufficient number of "red flags" before issuing the warning citation to support a reasonable suspicion of criminal activity and therefore justify extending the stop. When the officer first encountered the vehicle, he observed body language by both the driver and the defendant that he considered evasive; the driver exhibited extreme and continued nervousness throughout the stop and was unable to produce any form of personal identification; the driver and the defendant gave conflicting accounts of their travel plans and their relationship to each other; the officer observed an open sore on the defendant's face that appeared, based on the officer's training and experience, related to the use of methamphetamine; and background checks revealed that the driver had an expired license.

State v. Campola, 258 N.C. App. 292 (2018). The court ruled that an officer had reasonable suspicion to prolong a traffic stop. A six-year officer who had received training in identification of drugs pulled into the parking lot of a Motel 6, a high-crime area. When he entered the lot, he saw two men sitting in a car. After the officer passed, the vehicle exited the lot at high speed. The officer stopped the car after observing a traffic violation. The vehicle displayed a temporary license tag. When the officer approached for the driver's information, the driver was "more nervous than usual." The officer asked why the two men were at the motel, and the driver stated that they did not enter a room there. The passenger—the defendant—did not have any identifying documents but gave the officer his name. The officer went to his patrol car to enter the information in his computer and called for backup, as required by department regulations when more than one person is in a stopped vehicle. While waiting for backup to arrive, he entered the vehicle's VIN number in a fifty-state database, not having a state registration to enter. He determined that the vehicle was not stolen. Although neither the driver nor the passenger had outstanding warrants, both had multiple prior drug arrests. Shortly after, and twelve minutes after the stop began, the backup officer arrived. The two approached the vehicle some fourteen minutes after the stop was initiated. The stopping officer asked the driver to step out of and to the rear of the vehicle so that he and the backup officer could see the intersection where the traffic violation occurred. The stopping officer gave the driver a warning, returned his documents, and asked to search the vehicle. The driver declined. While the stopping officer was speaking with the driver, the backup officer approached the defendant and saw a syringe in the driver's seat. He asked the defendant to step out of the car and the defendant complied, at which point the officer saw a second syringe in the passenger seat. Four minutes into these conversations, the backup officer informed the stopping officer of the syringes. The stopping officer asked the driver if he was a diabetic, and the driver said that he was not. The stopping officer then searched the vehicle, finding the contraband at issue. On appeal, the court held that the stop was not improperly extended. It noted that the stopping officer was engaged in "conduct within the scope of his mission" until the backup officer arrived after twelve minutes. Database searches of driver's licenses, warrants, vehicle registrations, and proof of insurance all fall within the mission of a traffic stop. Additionally, the officer's research into the men's criminal histories was permitted as a precaution related to the traffic stop, as was the stopping officer's request for backup. Because officer safety stems from the mission of the traffic stop itself, time devoted to officer safety is time reasonably required to complete the mission of the stop. Even if a call for backup were not an appropriate safety precaution, here the backup call did not actually extend the stop because the stopping officer was still doing the required searches when the backup officer arrived. By the time the backup officer arrived, the stopping officer had developed a reasonable suspicion of criminal activity sufficient to extend the stop. The stopping officer was a trained officer who had participated in 100 drug arrests, he saw the driver and passenger in a high-crime area, after he drove by them they took off at a high speed and made an illegal turn, the driver informed the officer that the two were at the motel but did not go into a motel room, the driver was unusually nervous, and both men had multiple prior drug arrests. These facts provided reasonable suspicion to extend the stop. Even if these facts were insufficient, other facts supported a conclusion that reasonable suspicion existed, including the men's surprise at seeing the officer in the motel lot, the titling of the vehicle to someone other than the driver or passenger, the driver's statement that he met a friend at the motel but did not know the friend's name, and the officer's recognition of the defendant as someone who had been involved in illegal drug activity. Finally, drawing on some of the same facts, the court rejected the defendant's argument that any reasonable suspicion supporting extension of the stop was not particularized to him. The court also noted that an officer may stop and detain a vehicle and its occupants if the officer has reasonable suspicion that criminal activity is afoot.

State v. Bullock, 258 N.C. App. 72 (2018). On remand from the North Carolina Supreme Court, 370 N.C. 256 (2017), the court rejected the defendant's argument that his consent to search his rental vehicle was involuntary because it was given at a time when a traffic stop had been unduly prolonged. Specifically, the defendant argued that the stop was prolonged because of questioning by one officer and the time he was detained while waiting for a second officer to arrive to assist with the search. The case was before the court on remand from the state supreme court. That court had held that the initial traffic stop was valid, the officer lawfully frisked the defendant without prolonging the stop, the officer's database checks on the defendant's license did not unduly prolong the stop, and the conversation that occurred was sufficient to form reasonable suspicion authorizing the dog sniff of the vehicle and bag. Because all parts of the stop were lawfully extended, the trial court did not err in determining that the defendant's consent to search his vehicle was voluntary.

State v. Parker, 256 N.C. App. 319 (2017). Because the trial court's findings of fact did not support its conclusion that the defendant was legally seized at the time he consented to a search of his person, the court reversed the trial court's order denying the defendant's motion to suppress contraband found on his person. Officers were conducting surveillance on a known drug house. They noticed the defendant leave the residence in a truck and return twenty minutes later. He parked his truck in the driveway and walked towards a woman in the driveway of a nearby residence. The two began yelling at each other. Thinking the confrontation would escalate, the officers got out of their vehicle and separated the two. One officer asked the defendant for his identification. The officer checked the defendant's record, verifying that the defendant had no pending charges. Without returning the defendant's identification the officer then asked the defendant if he had any narcotics on him, and the defendant replied that he did not. At the officer's request, the defendant consented to a search of his person and vehicle. Drugs were found in his pants pocket. On appeal, the defendant argued that when the officer failed to return his identification after finding no outstanding warrants and after the initial reason for the detention was satisfied, the seizure became unlawful and the defendant's consent was not voluntary. The court agreed. It noted that the officer failed to return the defendant's identification before pursuing an inquiry into possession of drugs. It found that the trial court's order failed to provide findings of fact which would give rise to a reasonable suspicion that the defendant was otherwise subject to detention. Absent a reasonable suspicion to justify further delay, retaining the defendant's driver's license beyond the point of satisfying the initial purpose of the detention—de-escalating the conflict, checking the defendant's identification, and verifying that he had no outstanding warrants—was unreasonable. Thus, the defendant's consent to search his person, given during the period of unreasonable detention, was not voluntary.

FEDERAL APPELLATE COURTS (page 143)

United States v. Jordan, 952 F.3d 160 (4th Cir. 2020). This drug trafficking case arose from a prosecution in federal district court. Federal authorities apprehended another suspect involved in drugs, and that person became an informant, providing law enforcement with the defendant's name as a supplier. The informant agreed to call the defendant and set up a purchase. The phone call was recorded, and the two men discussed drug transactions using coded language. Based on that conversation, officers obtained search warrants for the defendant's phone and to authorize placement of a tracking device on the defendant's vehicle. Agents observed him make several quick visits to different locations, at times bringing one package into a location and leaving with a different package. The agents asked local police to conduct a traffic stop of the defendant based on these observations. The defendant ran a red light and was stopped by a Charlotte police officer. The defendant was on the phone and was "unwilling to engage" the officer. Multiple other cell phones were in view within the vehicle. The defendant was frisked, and a rubber glove was found in the defendant's pockets (an item the officer knew to be associated with drug trafficking). The defendant's brother appeared on the scene of the stop and tried to involve himself in the encounter. The officer waited eleven minutes for backup and then allowed a drug dog to check the vehicle. The dog alerted, and the defendant admitted to possessing cocaine. A search subsequently revealed cocaine, more than $25,000 in cash, six phones, and a gun. The defendant waived his Miranda rights and admitted his involvement in trafficking. Other drug stashes, guns, and large amounts of currency were found in the other places visited by the defendant on the day of the stop and at residences associated with him. The defendant moved to suppress evidence obtained as a result of the traffic stop, arguing that the stop was unreasonably extended in violation of *United States v. Rodriguez,* 575 U.S. 348 (2015).

The federal district court denied the motion, and the defendant was convicted at trial. A stop based on a traffic offense may not be extended beyond the time necessary to complete the mission of the stop absent reasonable suspicion of an offense or consent pursuant to *Rodriguez.* Here, the stopping officer was aware that the defendant was under investigation for trafficking drugs. Further, under the collective knowledge doctrine, all the information possessed by federal agents was imputed to the stopping officer. Based on the information from the informant, the search warrants that had issued, and the defendant's movements earlier in the day, law enforcement had reasonable suspicion of drug trafficking at the time of the stop. The suspicion of drug trafficking coupled with the presence of the defendant's brother on the scene justified the eleven-minute extension to wait for backup to arrive as a matter of officer safety. The stop was therefore not unconstitutionally extended, and the district court's denial of the motion to suppress was affirmed.

United States v. White, 836 F.3d 437 (4th Cir. 2016). A local West Virginia law enforcement officer stopped a car that had veered out of its lane. In addition to the driver, there was a front-seat passenger, the defendant, and one back-seat passenger, Bone. When approaching the driver's window, the officer smelled an odor of burned marijuana emanating from the car. The driver, whom the officer concluded was not impaired, denied knowledge of the marijuana. The officer requested that the defendant exit the car. When he did so, the officer asked him about the marijuana odor, but he denied that anything illegal was in the car. While talking with Bone, the officer saw a firearm in a piece of plastic molding on the front side of the passenger seat where the defendant had been sitting. The defendant was arrested and later convicted in federal district court of possession of a firearm by a felon.

The defendant conceded that the stop of the vehicle was supported by reasonable suspicion of a traffic violation under West Virginia law, but he contended that the officer unconstitutionally prolonged the stop. The fourth circuit noted that its case law provides that the odor of marijuana alone can provide probable cause to believe marijuana is present in a particular place. Thus, the officer had reasonable suspicion to extend the traffic stop to investigate the marijuana odor, and during that investigation the officer found the firearm. The court ruled that therefore the officer did not unconstitutionally prolong the traffic stop.

Scope of an Investigative Stop (page 143)

On page 146 of the main text, in the first case summarized in this section from the North Carolina Court of Appeals, *State v. Johnson*, the citation for the case summarized should be updated to read: *State v. Johnson*, 246 N.C. App. 677 (2016).

Ordering People Out of a Vehicle after a Lawful Stop (page 151)
NORTH CAROLINA SUPREME COURT (page 152)

State v. Bullock, 370 N.C. 256 (2017). The North Carolina Supreme Court reiterated that an officer may, as a matter of course, order a driver of a lawfully stopped vehicle to exit the vehicle.

When an Officer's Interaction with a Person Is a Seizure under the Fourth Amendment (page 154)
NORTH CAROLINA SUPREME COURT (page 156)

State v. Wilson, 370 N.C. 389 (2017). The state supreme court affirmed, per curiam and without an opinion, the ruling of the court of appeals, 250 N.C. App. 781 (2016), that the trial court properly denied the defendant's motion to suppress evidence obtained from his interaction with a police officer because no seizure occurred. The officer went to a residence to find a man who had outstanding warrants for his arrest. While walking towards the residence, the officer observed a pickup truck leaving. The officer waved his hands to tell the driver—the defendant—to stop. The officer intended to ask the defendant if he knew anything about the man with the outstanding warrants; the officer had no suspicion that the defendant was the man he was looking for or was engaged in criminal activity. The officer was in uniform but had no weapon drawn; his police vehicle was not blocking the road and neither his vehicle's blue lights nor sirens were activated. When the defendant stopped the vehicle, the officer almost immediately smelled an odor of alcohol from inside the vehicle. After the defendant admitted that he had been drinking, the officer arrested him for impaired driving. Because a reasonable person would have felt free to decline the officer's request to stop, no seizure occurred; rather, the encounter was consensual.

NORTH CAROLINA COURT OF APPEALS (page 157)

State v. Turnage, 259 N.C. App. 719 (2018). Citing *California v. Hodari D.,* 499 U.S. 621 (1991), the court noted that a show of authority by law enforcement does not constitute a seizure unless the suspect submits to that authority or is physically restrained. Here, for unknown reasons the driver of a van and the defendant stopped the vehicle in the middle of the road before any show of authority from law enforcement. A detective's later activation of blue lights did not constitute a seizure because the defendant did not yield to the show of authority. The defendant was not seized until the vehicle was stopped during a subsequent chase. Criminal activity observed by the detective during the chase and his observation of the two minor children in the van justified the arrest for fleeing to elude, resisting an officer, and child abuse.

State v. Burwell, 256 N.C. App. 722 (2017). The court ruled that an arrest occurs when, under G.S. 122C- 303, an officer takes a publicly intoxicated person to jail to assist that person and the action is taken against the person's will.

State v. Mangum, 250 N.C. App. 714 (2016). In this impaired-driving case, the court ruled that the defendant was not seized within the meaning of the Fourth Amendment until he submitted to an officer's authority by stopping his vehicle. The court rejected the defendant's argument that the seizure occurred when the officer activated his blue lights. Because the defendant continued driving after the blue lights were activated, there was no submission to the officer's authority and no seizure until the defendant stopped his vehicle. As a result, the reasonable suspicion inquiry can consider circumstances that arose after the officer's activation of his blue lights but before the defendant's submission to authority. The *Mangum* ruling was cited in *State v. Mahatha,* ___ N.C. App. ___, 832 S.E.2d 914 (2019), which concerned the defendant's conduct in not stopping after the officer's blue lights were activated and where the court concluded that, based on that conduct, the defendant's subsequent reckless and excessive speed provided the officer with reasonable suspicion to stop him.

The Authority to Make an Investigative Stop or Take Other Action without Reasonable Suspicion (page 161)

Detaining People Present When a Search Warrant Is Executed or Is Being Sought (page 161)

NORTH CAROLINA SUPREME COURT (page 162)

State v. Wilson, 371 N.C. 920, 921, 925, 921 (2018) (citation omitted). A SWAT team was sweeping a house so that the police could execute a search warrant. Several officers were positioned around the house to create a perimeter securing the scene. The defendant penetrated the SWAT perimeter, stating that he was going to get his moped. In so doing, he passed Officer Christian, who was stationed at the perimeter near the street. The defendant then kept going, moving up the driveway and towards the house to be searched. Officer Ayers, who was stationed near the house, confronted the defendant. After a brief interaction, Officer Ayers searched the defendant based on his suspicion that the defendant was armed. Officer Ayers found a firearm in the defendant's pocket. The defendant, who had previously been convicted of a felony, was arrested and charged with being a felon in possession of a firearm. He unsuccessfully moved to suppress evidence of the firearm at trial and was convicted.

The state supreme court held "that the rule in *Michigan v. Summers* [452 U.S. 692 (1981)] justifie[d] the seizure here because [the] defendant, who passed one officer, stated he was going to get his moped, and continued toward the premises being searched, posed a real threat to the safe and efficient completion of the search." The court interpreted the *Summers* rule to mean that a warrant to search for contraband founded on probable cause implicitly carries with it the limited authority to detain occupants who are within the immediate vicinity of the premises to be searched and who are present during the execution of a search warrant. Applying this rule, the court determined that "a person is an occupant for the purposes of the *Summers* rule if he 'poses a real threat to the safe and efficient execution of a search warrant.' " Here, the defendant posed such a threat. It reasoned: "He approached the house being swept, announced his intent to retrieve his moped from the premises, and appeared to be armed. It was obvious that [the] defendant posed a threat to the safe completion of the search."

Because the *Summers* rule only justifies detentions incident to the execution of search warrants, the court then considered whether the search of the defendant's person was justified. On this issue the court held that "both the search and seizure of the defendant were supported by individualized suspicion and thus did not violate the Fourth Amendment."

Conducting Impaired-Driving and Driver's License Checkpoints (page 162)
NORTH CAROLINA COURT OF APPEALS (page 164)

State v. Ashworth, 248 N.C. App. 649 (2016). In this impaired-driving case, the court ruled that the trial court erred by denying the defendant's motion to suppress evidence obtained from a checkpoint stop, which had asserted that the stop violated his constitutional rights. In a constitutional challenge to a checkpoint, a two-part inquiry applies: the court must first determine the primary programmatic purpose of the checkpoint; if a legitimate primary programmatic purpose is found, the court must judge its reasonableness. The defendant did not raise an issue about whether the checkpoint had a proper purpose. When determining reasonableness, a court must weigh the public's interest in the checkpoint against the individual's Fourth Amendment privacy interest, applying the *Brown v. Texas,* 443 U.S. 47 (1979), three-part test (gravity of the public concerns served by the seizure, the degree to which the seizure advances the public interest, and the severity of the interference with individual liberty) to this balancing inquiry. The court held that the trial court's findings of fact were insufficient to permit the trial court to meaningfully weigh the considerations required under the second and third prongs of the test. This constituted plain error. The court vacated the trial court's order denying the defendant's motion and remanded the case for further findings of fact and conclusions of law regarding the reasonableness of the checkpoint stop.

The Authority to Arrest: Probable Cause (page 172)
Determination of Probable Cause (page 172)
UNITED STATES SUPREME COURT (page 172)

Nieves v. Bartlett, 587 U.S. ___, 139 S. Ct. 1715 (2019). The Court held that because officers had probable cause to arrest plaintiff Bartlett, his First Amendment retaliatory arrest claim failed as a matter of law. Bartlett had sued the officers, alleging that they violated his First Amendment speech rights by arresting him for disorderly conduct and resisting arrest. The Court held that probable cause to make an arrest defeats a claim that the arrest was in retaliation for speech protected by the First Amendment.

District of Columbia v. Wesby, 583 U.S. ___, ___, 138 S. Ct. 577, 586 (2018) (citation omitted). In this civil suit against the District of Columbia and five of its police officers brought by individuals arrested for holding a raucous late-night party in a house they did not have permission to enter, the Court held that the officers had probable cause to arrest the partygoers and were entitled to qualified immunity. As to probable cause, the Court concluded that "[c]onsidering the totality of the circumstances, the officers made an 'entirely reasonable inference' that the partygoers were knowingly taking advantage of a vacant house as a venue for their late-night party." In this respect, the Court noted the condition of the house, including, among other things, that multiple neighbors told the officers that the house had been vacant for several months and that the house had virtually no furniture and few signs of inhabitance. The Court also noted the partygoers' conduct, including, among other things, that the party was still going strong when the officers arrived after 1:00 a.m., with music so loud that it could be heard from outside; upon entering, multiple officers smelled marijuana; partygoers had left beer bottles and cups of liquor on the floor; the living room had been converted into a makeshift strip club; and the officers found upstairs a group of men with a single, naked woman on a bare mattress—the only bed in the house—along with multiple open condom wrappers and a used condom. The Court further noted the partygoers' reaction to the officers, including scattering and hiding at the sight of the uniformed officers. Finally, the Court noted the partygoers' vague and implausible answers to the officers' questions about who had given them permission to be at the house. The Court went on to hold that the officers were entitled to qualified immunity.

NORTH CAROLINA SUPREME COURT (page 173)

State v. Parisi, 372 N.C. 639 (2019). The court ruled that the trial court erred by granting the defendant's motion to suppress evidence obtained as a result of his arrest by an officer in this impaired driving case. The court considered whether the trial court findings, which are conclusive on appeal if supported by competent evidence, supported its ultimate conclusion of law that an officer lacked probable cause to arrest the defendant for impaired driving. The trial court had made findings that the defendant admitted to consuming three beers, his eyes were red and glassy, a moderate odor of alcohol emanated from him, and he exhibited multiple indicia of impairment while performing various sobriety tests. The supreme court stated that it had "no hesitation" in concluding that these facts sufficed, as a matter of law, to establish probable cause for the officer's arrest of the defendant.

State v. Daniel, 372 N.C. 202 (2019). The supreme court, per curiam and without an opinion, affirmed the court of appeals ruling, 259 N.C. App. 334 (2018), that because an officer had probable cause to arrest the defendant for impaired driving, the trial court erred by granting the defendant's motion to suppress evidence obtained as a result of that arrest. Here, the trooper "clocked" the defendant traveling at 80 m.p.h. in a 65 m.p.h. zone. As the trooper approached the defendant's vehicle, the defendant abruptly moved from the left lane of the highway into the right lane, nearly striking another vehicle before stopping on the shoulder. During the stop, the trooper noticed a moderate odor of alcohol emanating from the defendant and observed an open 24-ounce container of beer in the cup-holder next to the driver's seat. The defendant told the trooper that he had just purchased the beer and was drinking it while driving down the highway. The defendant admitted that he had been drinking heavily several hours before the encounter with the trooper. The trooper did not have the defendant perform any field sobriety tests but did ask the defendant to submit to two Alco-sensor tests, both of which yielded positive results for alcohol. The court noted that while swerving alone does not give rise to probable cause, additional factors creating dangerous circumstances may, as was the case here.

NORTH CAROLINA COURT OF APPEALS (page 176)

State v. Fields, ___ N.C. App. ___, ___, 836 S.E.2d 886, 891 (2019). The court ruled that the trial court did not err in finding that an officer did not have probable cause to arrest the defendant for impaired driving. The court rejected the State's argument that certain findings of fact by the trial court were not supported by the evidence. In regard to the green pickup truck that the defendant was allegedly driving, the trial court found that the arresting officer testified that he did not see the truck park or see anyone get in or out of the truck. The State asserted that the officer testified that he observed a video at the mini mart where the truck was parked showing the defendant getting out of the truck. The court found that the officer testified that the video was lost because he left the flash drive containing the video in his patrol car when he took the car to a mechanic. The court ruled that the trial court determines the credibility of witnesses, the weight to be given to testimony, and reasonable inferences and that "[t]he trial court was free to give no weight to [the officer's] testimony regarding viewing the Mini-mart video." The court rejected the State's argument that probable cause existed to arrest the defendant for impaired driving. The court found that the trial judge's findings supported his conclusion that the State failed to show that the defendant was driving and, although the truck was registered to the defendant, failed to establish a connection between the driver of the truck and the defendant.

State v. Clapp, 259 N.C. App. 839 (2018). The court ruled that probable cause supported the defendant's second arrest for impaired driving. After the defendant's first arrest for DWI, he signed a written promise to appear and was released. Thirty minutes later, Officer Hall saw the defendant in the driver's seat of his vehicle at a gas station, with the engine running. The defendant had an odor of alcohol; slurred speech; red, glassy eyes; and was unsteady on his feet. The defendant told the officer that he was driving his vehicle to his son's residence. The officer did not perform field sobriety tests because the defendant was unable to safely stand on his feet. Based on the defendant's prior blood-alcohol reading—done less than two hours before the second incident—and the officer's training about the rate of alcohol elimination from the body, the officer formed the opinion that the defendant still had alcohol in his system. The defendant was arrested a second time for DWI and, because of his first arrest, also for driving while license revoked. The trial court granted the defendant's motion to suppress evidence obtained in connection with his second arrest. The State appealed, and the court of appeals reversed. The court began by determining that certain findings made by the trial court were not supported by competent evidence. The court then held that probable cause supported the defendant's second arrest. The defendant admitted that he drove his vehicle between his two encounters with the police. During the second encounter, Officer Hall observed that the defendant had red, glassy eyes; an odor of alcohol; slurred speech; and was unsteady on his feet to the extent that it was unsafe to conduct field sobriety tests. While Hall did not observe the defendant's driving behavior, he had personal knowledge that the defendant had a blood alcohol concentration of .16 one hour and forty minutes prior to the second encounter. And Hall testified that based on standard elimination rates of alcohol for an average individual, the defendant probably still would have been impaired.

State v. Wilkes, 256 N.C. App. 385 (2017). The court ruled that officers had probable cause to arrest the defendant and that, thus, the trial court did not err by denying the defendant's motion to suppress incriminating statements he made after his arrest. After law enforcement officers discovered a woman's body inside an abandoned, burned car, they arrested the defendant. During questioning after arrest, the defendant implicated himself in the woman's murder. He unsuccessfully moved to suppress those incriminating statements and challenged the trial court's denial of his suppression motion on appeal. At the time the officers arrested the defendant, they had already visited the victim's home and found a knife on a chair near a window with the screen cut. When they questioned the victim's boyfriend, he admitted that he was with the defendant at the victim's home on the night of the murder and that, after the victim locked the two men out of her house, the boyfriend cut the screen, entered the house through the window, unlocked the door from the inside, and let the defendant in. These facts and circumstances constituted sufficient information that would lead a reasonable officer to believe that the defendant had committed a breaking and entering. Thus, regardless of whether the officers had probable cause to arrest the defendant for murder, they had probable cause to arrest the defendant for that lesser crime.

State v. Messer, 255 N.C. App. 812 (2017). In this armed robbery and murder case, the court ruled that the trial court did not err by concluding that law enforcement officers had probable cause to arrest the defendant. Among other things, the defendant placed a telephone call using the victim's cell phone about twenty minutes before the victim's death was reported to law enforcement, the defendant spent the previous night at the victim's residence, the victim's son had last seen his father with the defendant, the victim's Smith and Wesson revolver was missing and a Smith and Wesson revolver was found near the victim's body, and the defendant was seen on the day of the victim's death driving an automobile matching the description of one missing from the victim's used car lot.

State v. Lindsey, 249 N.C. App. 516, 523 (2016). An officer had probable cause to arrest the defendant for DWI. After the officer stopped the defendant's vehicle, he smelled a moderate odor of alcohol coming from the defendant and noticed that the defendant's eyes were red and glassy. Upon administration of an HGN test (which tests for the involuntary jerking of a subject's eyes that is impacted by alcohol consumption), the officer observed five of six indicators of impairment. The defendant was unable to provide a breath sample for an Alco-Sensor, which the officer viewed as a willful refusal. The defendant admitted that he had consumed three beers, though he said his last consumption was nine hours prior. The officer arrested the defendant for DWI. The court stated: "Without even considering defendant's multiple failed attempts to provide an adequate breath sample on an [A]lco-sensor device, we hold the trial court's findings support its conclusion that there was probable cause to arrest defendant for DWI."

State v. Williams, 248 N.C. App. 112 (2016). An officer had probable cause to arrest the defendant for DWI. The officer responded to a call involving operation of a golf cart and serious injury to an individual.

The defendant admitted to the officer that he was the driver of the golf cart. The defendant had "very red and glassy" eyes and "a strong odor of alcohol coming from his breath." The defendant's clothes were bloody and he was very talkative, repeating himself several times. The defendant's mannerisms were "fairly slow" and he placed a hand on the officer's patrol car to maintain his balance. The defendant stated that he had "6 beers since noon" and submitted to an Alco-Sensor test, which was positive for alcohol.

Objective Standard in Determining Reasonable Suspicion, Probable Cause, or the Fact of Arrest (page 182)

NORTH CAROLINA SUPREME COURT (page 182)

State v. Nicholson, 371 N.C. 284 (2018). Finding that the court of appeals placed undue weight on an officer's subjective interpretation of the facts (the officer's testimony suggested that he did not believe he had reasonable suspicion of criminal activity) rather than focusing on how an objective, reasonable officer would have viewed them, the court noted that an action is reasonable under the Fourth Amendment, regardless of the officer's state of mind, if the circumstances viewed objectively justify the action.

The Arrest Procedure (page 185)

Entrance onto Premises to Arrest (page 186)

Exigent Circumstances (page 188)

NORTH CAROLINA COURT OF APPEALS (page 189)

State v. Adams, 250 N.C. App. 664, 671, 672 (2016). The court ruled that exigent circumstances justified officers' warrantless entry into the defendant's home to arrest him. It was undisputed that the officers had reasonable suspicion to stop the defendant for driving while license revoked. They pulled into the defendant's driveway behind him and activated blue lights as the defendant was exiting his vehicle and making his way towards his front door. The defendant did not stop for the blue lights and continued hurriedly towards the front door after the officers told him to stop. "At that point," the court explained, "the officers had probable cause to arrest defendant for resisting a public officer and began a 'hot pursuit' of defendant." The officers arrived at the front door just as the defendant was making his way across the threshold and were able to prevent him from closing the door. The officers then forced the front door open and detained and arrested the defendant just inside the door. The court held that the warrantless entry and arrest was proper under *United States v. Santana,* 427 U.S. 38 (1976). It explained: "Hot pursuit has been recognized as an exigent circumstance sufficient to justify a warrantless entry [into a residence where] there is probable cause without consideration of immediate danger or destruction of evidence."

Chapter 3

Law of Search and Seizure

Introduction (page 195)

Footnote 3 (page 195)

In *State v. Terrell*,[1] the North Carolina Supreme Court ruled that an officer's warrantless search of a defendant's thumb drive following a prior search by a private person violated the defendant's Fourth Amendment rights. While examining the thumb drive, the defendant's girlfriend saw an image of her 9-year-old sleeping granddaughter exposed from the waist up. Believing the image was inappropriate, the girlfriend contacted the sheriff's office and turned over the thumb drive. Later, a detective conducted a warrantless search of the thumb drive to locate the image in question, during which he discovered other images of what he believed to be child pornography before he found the photograph of the granddaughter. The detective then applied for and obtained a warrant to search the contents of the thumb drive for "contraband images of child pornography and evidence of additional victims and crimes."[2] The initial warrant application relied only on information from the defendant's girlfriend, but after the State Bureau of Investigation requested additional information, the detective included information about the images he found in his initial search of the USB drive.

The supreme court concluded that the girlfriend opening the thumb drive and viewing some of its contents did not frustrate the defendant's privacy interest in the entire contents of the device. To the contrary, digital devices can retain massive amounts of information, organized into files that are essentially containers within containers. Because the trial court did not make findings establishing the precise scope of the girlfriend's search, it likewise could not find that the detective had the level of "virtual certainty" contemplated by *United States v. Jacobsen*, 466 U.S. 109 (1984), that the device contained nothing else of significance, or that a later search would not tell him anything more than he already had been told. The search therefore was not permissible under the private-search doctrine. The court affirmed the decision of the court of appeals and remanded the case for consideration of whether the search warrant would have been supported by probable cause without the evidence obtained through the unlawful search.

Observations and Actions That May Not Implicate Fourth Amendment Rights (page 196)

NEW SECTION: Searches of Stolen or Misappropriated Property

A person does not have a reasonable expectation of privacy in stolen property and so cannot contest an officer's search of such property.[3] However, the United States Supreme Court recently ruled that a person driving a rental car may have a reasonable expectation of privacy in the vehicle even if the person is not listed as an

---

1. 372 N.C. 657 (2019), *aff'g* 257 N.C. App. 884 (2018).

2. *Id.* at 659.

3. *See, e.g.,* State v. White, 311 N.C. 238, 244 (1984) (citation omitted) ("Defendant also challenges the search of the vehicle by law enforcement officers without a warrant. The record discloses that the vehicle in question was in fact stolen. Defendant presented no evidence showing any legitimate property or possessory interest in the automobile. The law is well settled in this jurisdiction that one has no standing to 'object to a search or seizure of the premises or property of another.' ").

authorized driver on the rental agreement; such a person is not necessarily in the same position as a thief. In *Byrd v. United States*,[4] the Court considered a driver who had been entrusted with a vehicle by a friend who was the only person listed on the rental agreement. The Court stated that "as a general rule, someone in otherwise lawful possession and control of a rental car has a reasonable expectation of privacy in it even if the rental agreement does not list him or her as an authorized driver."[5] Such a person would have a "right to exclude" others from the vehicle, such as potential carjackers, and would be able to contest a law enforcement search of the vehicle.[6]

Areas Outside the Home: Curtilage and Open Fields (page 200)

The Curtilage (page 200)

The North Carolina Court of Appeals in *State v. Degraphenreed*[7] ruled that a car parked on the side of a public street opposite to the defendant's residence and outside the confines of the fence surrounding the residence was not within the residence's curtilage.

Common Entranceway to Residence (page 203)

In *State v. Stanley*,[8] the court of appeals ruled that officers violated the Fourth Amendment by conducting a knock and talk at the back door of a residence, even though a gravel driveway "led to the back of the apartment" and a confidential informant had used the back door three times to make controlled buys at the property. The court emphasized that the front door is the entry normally used by social visitors, and stated that only in "unusual circumstances," not present here, would an officer be justified in approaching a side door or back door for a knock and talk. Although the informant used the back door several times, "the fact that the resident of a home may choose to allow certain individuals to use a back or side door does not mean that similar permission is deemed to have been given generally to members of the public."[9] The court's statements regarding the usual impermissibility of approaching a side door to a residence may call into question the suggestion in the final paragraph of this section of the main text that ordinarily a knock and talk may be conducted at either a front or a side door.

---

4. 584 U.S. ___, 138 S. Ct. 1518 (2018).

5. *Id.* at ___, 138 S. Ct. at 1524.

6. For a complete discussion of *Byrd*, see Jeff Welty, *Supreme Court: Driver of Rental Car, Not Listed on Rental Agreement, Has Reasonable Expectation of Privacy*, UNC Sch. of Gov't: N.C. Crim. L. Blog (May 21, 2018), https://nccriminallaw.sog.unc.edu/supreme-court-driver-of-rental-car-not-listed-on-rental-agreement-has-reasonable-expectation-of-privacy/.

7. 261 N.C. App. 235 (2018).

8. 259 N.C. App. 708, 709, 718, 717 (2018). *See also* State v. Ellis, ___ N.C. App. ___, 829 S.E.2d 912 (2019) (detectives were not permitted to roam the curtilage of the residential property searching for something or someone after attempting a failed knock and talk at front door); State v. Piland, 263 N.C. App. 323 (2018) (officers conducting a knock and talk can lawfully approach residence as long as they remain within the permissible scope afforded by a knock and talk; here, given the configuration of the property, any private person wishing to knock on the defendant's front door would have to drive into the driveway, get out, walk between the car and the path so as to stand next to the garage, and continue on the path to the front porch).

9. 259 N.C. App. at 717.

Plain View Sensory Perceptions (Observation, Smell, Sound, Touch, and Taste) (page 203)
Use of Special Devices or Animals (page 207)

Aircraft (page 207)

Law enforcement agencies are increasingly relying on drones, rather than traditional aircraft, to conduct aerial overflights and surveillance. North Carolina statutory law requires an officer to obtain a warrant before using a drone to conduct surveillance of a person, a dwelling, or curtilage absent consent or exigency.[10]

Dogs (page 209)

Although the use of a dog during a traffic stop is not itself a search and does not itself invade a motorist's reasonable expectation of privacy, it is important to remember that, under *Rodriguez v. United States*,[11] the use of the dog may not extend the duration of the stop absent consent or reasonable suspicion.

Wiretapping, Eavesdropping, Access to Stored Electronic Communications, and Related Issues (page 210)

Access to Real-Time (Prospective) or Historical Cell-Site Location Information (page 220)

The United States Supreme Court ruled in *Carpenter v. United States*[12] that "when the Government accessed [many days' worth of historical cell-site location information] from [a suspect's] wireless carriers, it invaded [his] reasonable expectation of privacy in the whole of his physical movements," and so conducted a search for purposes of the Fourth Amendment. The Court stated that investigators "must generally obtain a warrant supported by probable cause before acquiring such records,"[13] unless an exception to the warrant requirement is present, such as exigency. This effectively overruled the *Perry* decision noted in the main volume, as well as the similar decisions of many other lower courts.[14] It also effectively prohibits officers from using a "reasonable grounds" court order under 18 U.S.C. § 2703(d) to obtain long-term historical cell-site location information.

Carpenter does not address all the legal issues concerning cell phones and location information. The majority in the case expressly declined to opine about the Fourth Amendment status of "real-time CSLI [(cell-site location information)] or 'tower dumps,'" and left open the possibility that obtaining only short-term historical

---

10. *See* G.S. 15A-300.1. For a discussion of the various legal constraints and considerations involved in law enforcement use of drones, see Jeff Welty, *Update on Drones*, UNC Sch. of Gov't: N.C. Crim. L. Blog (Aug. 22, 2017), https://nccriminallaw.sog.unc.edu/update-on-drones/.

11. 575 U.S. 348 (2015).

12. 585 U.S. ___, ___, 138 S. Ct. 2206, 2219 (2018).

13. *Id.* at ___, 138 S. Ct. at 2221. *See* State v. Gore, ___ N.C. App. ___, 846 S.E.2d 295 (2020) (pre-*Carpenter*, officer obtained historical cell-site location information with a "reasonable grounds" court order; court of appeals ruled that under the good-faith exception to the exclusionary rule under the U.S. Constitution (applicable when an officer acts with an "objectively reasonable belief" that his or her actions do not violate the Fourth Amendment), the information was properly admitted at trial under the federal constitution; court also ruled that the information was properly admitted under the North Carolina Constitution because the judge who issued the court order specifically found "probable cause" to issue it, so the order was the functional equivalent of a search warrant).

14. *See, e.g.,* United States v. Riley, 858 F.3d 1012, 1013 (6th Cir. 2017) (ruling that "tracking [a robbery defendant's] real-time GPS location data for approximately seven hours preceding his arrest . . . did not amount to a Fourth Amendment search" and therefore did not require probable cause).

CSLI would not be a search.[15] A cautious officer seeking CSLI or other phone-related location information, even information not directly governed by the holding in *Carpenter,* may wish to use a search warrant or the functional equivalent, such as a court order based on full probable cause, to do so.[16]

Bank Records (page 222)

The North Carolina State Bar has determined that only a prosecutor, not an officer, may file a motion with a court for an order seeking financial records. The State Bar cautioned an officer who filed such a motion, concluding that the officer engaged in the unauthorized practice of law by doing so.[17]

Search and Seizure by Valid Consent (page 224)
Content of a Valid Consent (page 229)
Voluntariness of the Expression (page 229)

If a person has been unlawfully detained, any consent to search given during the unlawful detention is likely to be deemed invalid, either as involuntary or as tainted fruit of the detention.[18]

Invasion of Privacy by a Search or Seizure with Sufficient Reason (page 233)
Search and Seizure of Evidence with Probable Cause (page 234)
Search and Seizure of Vehicles with Probable Cause (page 236)

In *Collins v. Virginia,*[19] the United States Supreme Court ruled that the automobile exception to the warrant requirement does not permit an officer, uninvited and without a warrant, to enter the curtilage of a home to search a vehicle parked there. The Court stated that "the scope of the automobile exception extends no further than the automobile itself."[20] It rejected Virginia's request that it expand the scope of the automobile exception to permit police to access an automobile to carry out a search even if the Fourth Amendment protects the area through which the officer would need to travel to reach the vehicle:

---

15. *Carpenter,* 585 U.S. at ___, 138 S. Ct. at 2220. For a detailed discussion of *Carpenter,* see Jeff Welty, *Supreme Court Rules That Obtaining Cell Site Location Information Is a Search,* UNC SCH. OF GOV'T: N.C. CRIM. L. BLOG (June 25, 2018), https://nccriminallaw.sog.unc.edu/9411-2/.

16. For a further discussion of whether a court order based on probable cause may be used in place of a search warrant, see Jeff Welty, *Carpenter, Search Warrants, and Court Orders Based on Probable Cause,* UNC SCH. OF GOV'T: N.C. CRIM. L. BLOG (July 30, 2018), https://nccriminallaw.sog.unc.edu/carpenter-search-warrants-and-court-orders-based-on-probable-cause/. See the discussion of a court order versus a search warrant in *Gore,* ___ N.C. ___, 846 S.E.2d 295.

17. For a complete discussion of the unauthorized practice issue, and to see a copy of the State Bar's letter, see Jeff Welty, *Officers' Applications for Investigative Orders and the Unauthorized Practice of Law,* UNC SCH. OF GOV'T: N.C. CRIM. L. BLOG (May 7, 2018), https://nccriminallaw.sog.unc.edu/officers-applications-for-investigative-orders-and-the-unauthorized-practice-of-law/.

18. *See* Florida v. Royer, 460 U.S. 491, 507–08 (1983) ("Because . . . Royer was being illegally detained when he consented to the search of his luggage . . . the consent was tainted by the illegality and was ineffective to justify the search."); State v. Parker, 256 N.C. App. 319, 327 (2017) (ruling that "defendant's consent to search his person, given during the period of unreasonable detention, was not voluntary").

19. 584 U.S. ___, 138 S. Ct. 1663 (2018).

20. *Id.* at ___, 138 S. Ct. at 1667.

Just as an officer must have a lawful right of access to any contraband he discovers in plain view in order to seize it without a warrant, and just as an officer must have a lawful right of access in order to arrest a person in his home, so, too, an officer must have a lawful right of access to a vehicle in order to search it pursuant to the automobile exception. The automobile exception does not afford the necessary lawful right of access to search a vehicle parked within a home or its curtilage because it does not justify an intrusion on a person's separate and substantial Fourth Amendment interest in his home and curtilage.[21]

Search of a Person for Evidence with Probable Cause (page 245)

Probable cause to arrest and to search (page 245)

In *State v. Pigford*,[22] the defendant was driving a vehicle that was stopped at a checkpoint. A passenger was sitting in the front seat. The officer smelled an odor of marijuana coming from the vehicle but was unable to establish the exact location of the odor. The officer ordered the defendant out of the vehicle and searched him, finding cocaine and other items. The state court of appeals found the search of the defendant unjustified, as there was no evidence that the odor was personally attributable to the defendant. When an officer smells an odor of marijuana coming from a vehicle, the vehicle itself may be searched under the automobile exception to the warrant requirement, but the odor does not automatically provide an officer with probable cause to conduct an immediate warrantless search of the driver.[23]

Obtaining a blood sample when an impaired driver refuses a chemical test or is unconscious[24] (page 245)

The North Carolina Court of Appeals applied *McNeely* in *State v. Burris*,[25] finding sufficient exigency to support a warrantless blood draw. The defendant refused to take a breath test during an encounter with an officer, and the officer estimated that it would take an hour and a half to get a search warrant given the limited number of officers available to assist and the distance to the magistrate's office. A roadside test had indicated that the defendant's blood-alcohol concentration was .10, so the officer reasonably believed that the delay would result in the dissipation of alcohol in the defendant's blood.

What if a defendant is unable to refuse to give a blood sample because the defendant is unconscious? In *Mitchell v. Wisconsin*,[26] the United States Supreme Court ruled[27] that when an officer has probable cause to believe that a person has committed an impaired driving offense and the person's unconsciousness or stupor requires the person to be taken to the hospital before a breath test may be performed, the State may "almost always"[28] order a warrantless blood test based on exigent circumstances to measure the driver's blood-alcohol concentration without violating the Fourth Amendment.[29]

---

21. *Id.* at ___, 138 S. Ct. at 1672.

22. 248 N.C. App. 797 (2016).

23. For a further discussion of *Pigford* and other cases concerning searches of vehicles and their occupants based on an officer's detection of the odor of marijuana, see Jeff Welty, *Searches of Vehicles and Occupants Based on the Odor of Marijuana*, UNC SCH. OF GOV'T: N.C. CRIM. L. BLOG (Sept. 19, 2016), https://nccriminallaw.sog.unc.edu/searches-vehicles-occupants-based-odor-marijuana/.

24 The words "or is unconscious" have been added to the title of this subsection.

25. 253 N.C. App. 525 (2017).

26. 588 U.S. ___, 139 S. Ct. 2525 (2019).

27. The four-Justice plurality opinion announcing the judgment of the court is binding on lower courts based on the ruling in *Marks v. United States*, 430 U.S. 188 (1977), because the opinion was based on narrower grounds than those cited by the fifth Justice, who concurred in the judgment but wrote a separate opinion.

28. 588 U.S. at ___, 139 S. Ct. at 2531.

29. *Author's note*: The Fourth Amendment ruling in *State v. Romano*, 369 N.C. 678 (2017) (taking of blood in DWI investigation from unconscious defendant was not supported by exigent circumstances), decided before *Mitchell*, does not appear to comport with the *Mitchell* exigency test. See the discussion of *Mitchell* and *Romano* in Shea Denning, *Supreme Court Announces New Exigency Test for Blood Draws from Unconscious*

Search and Seizure to Protect Officers, Other People, or Property (page 249)
Search Incident to Arrest (page 249)

Strip searches and body-cavity searches (page 253)

In *State v. Fuller*,[30] the North Carolina Court of Appeals ruled that a search of the defendant's person was a proper search incident to his arrest. An officer stopped the defendant's vehicle for driving with a revoked license and arrested the defendant. The officer then conducted a consent search of the vehicle, which failed to locate any contraband. However, a K-9 dog arrived and "hit" on the driver's seat cushion. When a further search uncovered no contraband or narcotics, the officer concluded that the narcotics must be on the defendant's person. The defendant was brought to the police department and was searched. The search involved lowering the defendant's pants and long johns to his knees. During the search the officer pulled out, but did not pull down, the defendant's underwear and observed the defendant's genitals and buttocks. Cocaine eventually was retrieved from a hidden area on the fly of the defendant's pants. The court of appeals rejected the defendant's argument that the strip search could only have been conducted with probable cause and exigent circumstances, noting that the exigency standard applies only to roadside strip searches. Here, the search was conducted incident to the defendant's lawful arrest and inside a private interview room at a police facility. Furthermore, the scope of the search was reasonable. It was limited to the area of the defendant's body and clothing that would have come in contact with the cushion of the driver's seat where the dog alerted, and the defendant was searched inside a private interview room at the police station with only the defendant and two officers present. The officers did not remove the defendant's clothing above the waist. They did not fully remove his undergarments, nor did they touch his genitals or any body cavity. The court thus concluded that the place, manner, justification, and scope of the search of the defendant's person were reasonable.

Frisk of a Person for Weapons (page 257)

Discovering evidence during a frisk; plain touch (feel) doctrine (page 258)
Footnote 423 (page 259)

Add the following case to this footnote: State v. Johnson, ___ N.C. App. ___, 837 S.E.2d 179 (2019) (while conducting a pat-down of the defendant, the officer felt a soft, rubbery wad in his pocket that the officer immediately believed to be narcotics packaged in plastic baggies; the court ruled that the counterfeit drugs were admissible under the "plain feel" doctrine).

Entry or Search of a Home to Render Emergency Assistance or for Self-Protection (page 260)

Protective sweep when officer is in a home to make an arrest (page 261)

Add a footnote after the first sentence in this section, with note text reading as follows: "Maryland v. Buie, 494 U.S. 325 (1990); State v. Smith, 371 N.C. 469 (2018) (reversing decision of court of appeals based on the reasons stated in dissenting opinion, 255 N.C. App. 138 (2017))."

DWI Suspects, UNC SCH. OF GOV'T: N.C. CRIM. LAW BLOG (July 9, 2019), https://nccriminallaw.sog.unc.edu/supreme-court-announces-new-exigency-test-for-blood-draws-from-unconscious-dwi-suspects/.
   30. 257 N.C. App. 181 (2017).

Chapter 3 Appendix: Case Summaries

Search and Seizure Issues (page 275)

What Is a Search and Seizure and What Evidence May Be Searched for and Seized (page 275)

Definition of a Search (page 275)

NORTH CAROLINA SUPREME COURT (page 277)

State v. Grady, 372 N.C. 509 (2019). The court ruled that the satellite-based monitoring (SBM) of sex offenders violates the Fourth Amendment as applied to any unsupervised person who was ordered to enroll in SBM solely because the person is a recidivist. By unsupervised, the court meant a person not on probation, parole, or post-release supervision. For a detailed analysis of this case, see Jamie Markham, *Satellite-Based Monitoring Is Unconstitutional for All Unsupervised Recidivists,* UNC Sch. of Gov't: N.C. Crim. L. Blog (Sept. 12, 2019), nccriminallaw.sog.unc.edu/satellite-based-monitoring-is-unconstitutional-for-all-unsupervised-recidivists/.

Observations and Actions That May Not Implicate Fourth Amendment Rights (page 280)

Private Search or Seizure (page 280)

NORTH CAROLINA SUPREME COURT (page 280)

State v. Terrell, 372 N.C. 657, 659 (2019). The court ruled that an officer's warrantless search of a defendant's thumb drive following a prior search by a private individual violated the defendant's Fourth Amendment rights. While examining a thumb drive belonging to the defendant, the defendant's girlfriend saw an image of her 9-year-old granddaughter sleeping, exposed from the waist up. Believing the image was inappropriate, the girlfriend contacted the sheriff's office and gave them the thumb drive. Later, a detective conducted a warrantless search of the thumb drive to locate the image in question, during which he discovered other images of what he believed to be child pornography before he found the photograph of the granddaughter. At that point the detective applied for and obtained a warrant to search the contents of the thumb drive for "contraband images of child pornography and evidence of additional victims and crimes." The initial warrant application relied only on information from the defendant's girlfriend, but after the State Bureau of Investigation (SBI) requested additional information, the detective included information about the images he found in his initial search of the USB drive. The SBI's forensic examination turned up twelve images, ten of which had been deleted and archived in a way that would not have been viewable without special forensic capabilities.

The court concluded that the girlfriend opening the thumb drive and viewing some of its contents did not frustrate the defendant's privacy interest in the entire contents of the device. To the contrary, digital devices can retain massive amounts of information, organized into files that are essentially containers within containers. Because the trial court did not make findings establishing the precise scope of the girlfriend's search, it likewise could not find that the detective had the level of "virtual certainty" contemplated by *United States v. Jacobsen*, 466 U.S. 109 (1984), that the device contained nothing else of significance or that a subsequent search would not tell him anything more than he already had been told. The search therefore was not permissible under the private-search doctrine. The court affirmed the decision of the court of appeals, 257 N.C. App. 884 (2018), and remanded the case for consideration of whether the warrant would have been supported by probable cause without the evidence obtained through the unlawful search.

Abandoned Property and Garbage (page 282)

United States v. Small, 944 F.3d 490, 502, 503 (4th Cir. 2019) (citations omitted). The defendant was convicted in federal district court of charges of federal carjacking and related offenses. The defendant robbed a victim of a car at gunpoint. That car was located three days later, with the defendant driving it. When officers tried to apprehend the defendant, he led them on a high-speed chase that ended when he crashed the vehicle into the fence at Fort Meade, Maryland. The defendant fled on foot and evaded police throughout the night but was located and arrested in the morning. During the search the night before, officers located items discarded by the defendant, including his cell phone, shirt, and hat. Law enforcement noticed that the cell phone had missed calls from a number identified on the phone as "Sincere my Wife." An officer called that number back and determined that the defendant was the likely owner of the phone. Later that morning, officers again used the phone to contact "Sincere," answered one of her calls, and recorded the phone's serial number. The government later obtained search warrants to obtain (1) the phone's historical cell-site location data and all of its calls, texts, and Internet history and (2) records on another phone that was in contact with the defendant's phone on the date of the offenses with which the defendant was charged. The records produced pursuant to those warrants incriminated the defendant and a co-defendant. The defendant moved to suppress the evidence that resulted from the warrantless searches of his phone. The district court denied the motion, finding that the phone had been abandoned. The defendant was convicted at trial, and the fourth circuit affirmed the district court's ruling.

Under *Abel v. United States,* 362 U.S. 217 (1960), a person has no reasonable expectation of privacy in abandoned property. Property that is merely lost is not abandoned. There must be some voluntary action by the defendant that supports finding that the defendant renounced his interest in the property. The fourth circuit stated:

> A finding of abandonment is based "not [on] whether all formal property rights have been relinquished, but whether the complaining party retains a reasonable expectation of privacy in the articles alleged to be abandoned." To determine whether the defendant maintains a reasonable expectation of privacy in an item, the court performs "an objective analysis" which considers the defendant's actions and intentions.

Here, the defendant left the cell phone in the area where he crashed the car he was driving, along with the vehicle, its contents, his shirt, and his hat. He was actively fleeing police and likely discarded the items to avoid detection. The cell phone was found within 50 feet of the defendant's bloody shirt. The phone was found in a grassy area, away from "a place where [someone] normally might be," and this indicated that the defendant intended to discard it. A rational defendant might well decide to abandon the phone, given the potential for cell-phone tracking. While it was possible that the defendant might have lost his phone, it was unlikely under these facts. "[W]hile phones occasionally slip out of pockets, shirts do not accidentally fall off their wearers—at the exact same moment as hats—and cars do not ditch themselves after a crash." These circumstances amply supported abandonment, and the motion to suppress the cell phone evidence was properly denied.

United States v. Lyles, 910 F.3d 787, 790, 792, 794, 796, 797 (4th Cir. 2018). Maryland police discovered the defendant's phone number in the contacts of a homicide victim's phone. Suspecting the defendant's involvement, law enforcement conducted a "trash pull" and searched four bags of the defendant's garbage after they were placed on the curb. Police found "three unknown type plant stems [which later tested positive for marijuana], three empty packs of rolling papers," and mail addressed to the residence. A search warrant for evidence of drug possession, drug distribution, guns, and money laundering was obtained on that basis. The warrant authorized the search of the defendant's home for any drugs; firearms; documents and records of nearly any kind; and various electronic equipment, including cell phones. It also authorized the search of all persons and cars. Guns, ammunition, marijuana, and drug paraphernalia were found, and the defendant was charged with possession of a firearm by a felon. The federal district court suppressed the evidence, finding that the evidence from the garbage search did not establish probable cause that more drugs would be found within the home. The trial judge declined to apply the good-faith exception to the exclusionary rule set out in *United States v. Leon*, 468 U.S. 897, 918 (1984) ("provid[ing] an exception . . . when 'officers acted in the objectively reasonable belief that their conduct did not violate the Fourth Amendment' "), finding that the warrant here was "plainly overbroad." The government appealed.

The fourth circuit affirmed. It noted that *California v. Greenwood*, 486 U.S. 35 (1988), allows the warrantless search of curbside garbage. The practice is an important technique for law enforcement, but it is also "subject to abuse" by its very nature—guests may leave garbage at a residence that ends up on the street; evidence can easily be planted in curbside garbage. The court stated:

> The open and sundry nature of trash requires that [items found from a trash pull] be viewed with at least modest circumspection. Moreover, it is anything but clear that a scintilla of marijuana residue or hint of marijuana use in a trash can should support a sweeping search of the residence.

The government argued that the warrant at least supplied probable cause for drug possession and that anything else seen in the course of the execution of the warrant was properly within plain view. In its view, a single marijuana stem would always provide probable cause to search a residence for drugs. The fourth circuit disagreed:

> The government invites the court to infer from the trash pull evidence that additional drugs probably would have been found in [the defendant's] home. Well perhaps, but not probably. . . . This was a single trash pull, and thus less likely to reveal evidence of recurrent or ongoing activity. And from that one trash pull, as defendant argues, "the tiny quantity of discarded residue gives no indication of how long ago marijuana may have been consumed in the home." This case is almost singular in the sparseness of evidence pulled in one instance from the trash itself and the absence of other evidence to corroborate even that.

The court therefore found that the magistrate lacked a substantial basis on which to find probable cause and unanimously reversed. The opinion also noted the breadth of the search. The warrant was "astonishingly broad"—it authorized the search of items "wholly unconnected with marijuana possession." This was akin to a general warrant and unreasonable for such a "relatively minor" offense.

The court also rejected the application of the *Leon* good-faith exception to save the warrant, despite the fact that the warrant application was reviewed by the officer's superior and a prosecutor. "The prosecutor's and supervisor's review, while unquestionably helpful, 'cannot be regarded as dispositive' of the good faith inquiry. If it were, police departments might be tempted to immunize warrants through perfunctory superior review . . ." Concluding, the court stated: "What we have here is a flimsy trash pull that produced scant evidence of a marginal offense but that nonetheless served to justify the indiscriminate rummaging through a household. Law enforcement can do better."

Areas outside the Home: Curtilage and Open Fields (page 287)
UNITED STATES SUPREME COURT (page 287)

Collins v. Virginia, 584 U.S. ___, ___, 138 S. Ct. 1663, 1670–71 (2018). In the course of deciding whether an officer's warrantless search of a motorcycle parked in the driveway of a home was justified under the automobile exception, the Court considered whether the motorcycle was parked within the curtilage of the dwelling. It ruled that it was. The motorcycle was parked at the end of the driveway, which terminated next to the house. The parking area was "enclosed on two sides by a brick wall about the height of a car and on a third side by the house. A side door provide[d] direct access between this partially enclosed section of the driveway and the house. A visitor endeavoring to reach the front door of the house would have to walk partway up the driveway, but would turn off before entering the enclosure and instead proceed up a set of steps leading to the front porch." On these facts, the Court had no difficulty concluding that the motorcycle was parked within the curtilage.

NORTH CAROLINA COURT OF APPEALS (page 290)

State v. Ellis, ___ N.C. App. ___, ___, 829 S.E.2d 912, 916, 918 (2019). After discovering stolen property at a home across the street, two officers approached the front door of the defendant's residence after being informed by a witness that the person who stole the property was at the residence. One of the officers knocked on the front door but no one answered. He observed a large spiderweb in the door frame. After knocking for several minutes, the officer observed a window curtain inside the home move. The other officer went to the back of the home. No one answered that officer's knock at the back door either, despite the fact that he also knocked for several minutes. He then left the back door and approached the left front corner of the home, where he smelled marijuana. The other officer confirmed the smell, and both officers observed a fan loudly blowing from the crawl space area of the home. The odor of marijuana was emanating from the fan, and one of the officers looked between the fan slats, where he observed marijuana plants. A search warrant was obtained on this basis, and the defendant was charged with trafficking marijuana and other drug offenses.

The trial court denied the defendant's motion to suppress evidence obtained from the search, finding that the smell and sight of the marijuana plants were in plain view. The court of appeals reversed. *Florida v. Jardines*, 569 U.S. 1 (2013), recognizes the importance of the home in the Fourth Amendment context and limits the authority of officers conducting a knock and talk. *Jardines* found that a search had occurred when officers conducting a knock and talk used a drug-sniffing dog on the suspect's front porch and that such action exceeded the permissible boundaries of a knock and talk. Even though no police dog was present here, the court of appeals, citing *Jardines*, found that "[t]he detectives were not permitted to roam the property searching for something or someone after attempting a failed 'knock and talk.' Without a warrant, they could only 'approach the home by the front path, knock promptly, and then (absent invitation to linger longer) leave.'" North Carolina applies the *Jardines* home protections to the curtilage of the property, and the officers here exceeded their authority by moving about the curtilage without a warrant. Once the knocks at the front door went unanswered, the officers should have left. The court discounted the State's argument that the lack of a "no trespassing" sign on the defendant's property meant that the officers could be present in and around the yard of the home. In the words of the court:

> While the evidence of a posted no trespassing sign may be evidence of a lack of consent, nothing . . . supports the State's attempted expansion of the argument that the lack of such a sign is tantamount to an invitation for someone to enter and linger in the curtilage of the residence.

Because the officers here only smelled the marijuana after leaving the front porch and lingering in the curtilage, they were not in a position in which they could be lawfully, and the plain view exception to the Fourth Amendment did not apply. Even if the officers were lawfully present in the yard, the defendant had a reasonable expectation of privacy in his crawl space area, and the officers violated that by looking through the fan slats.

State v. Piland, 263 N.C. App. 323, 326, 333 (2018). In this drug case, the court ruled that the trial court did not err by denying the defendant's motion to suppress. After receiving a tip that the defendant was growing marijuana at his home, three officers drove there for a knock and talk. They pulled into the driveway and parked in front of the defendant's car, which was parked at the far end of the driveway, beside the home. The garage was located immediately to the left of the driveway. One officer went to the front door to knock, while the other two remained by the garage. A strong odor of marijuana was coming from the garage area. On the defendant's front door was a sign reading "inquiries" and listing his phone number, and a second sign reading "warning" and citing several statutes. As soon as the defendant opened the front door, the knocking officer smelled marijuana. The officer decided to "maintain the residence pending the issuance of a search warrant." After the warrant was obtained, a search revealed drugs and drug paraphernalia.

The court began by rejecting the defendant's argument that the officers engaged in an unconstitutional search and seizure by being present in his driveway and lingering by his garage. Officers conducting a knock and talk can lawfully approach a home so long as they remain within the permissible scope afforded by the knock and talk. Here, given the configuration of the property, any private citizen wishing to knock on the defendant's front door would drive into the driveway, get out, walk between the car and the path so as to stand next to the garage, and continue on the path to the front porch. Therefore, the officers' conduct, in pulling into the driveway by the garage, getting out of their car, and standing between the car and the garage was permitted. Additionally, the officers were allowed to linger by the garage while their colleague approached the front door. Thus, "the officers' lingering by the garage was justified and did not constitute a search under the Fourth Amendment."

The court then ruled that by failing to raise the issue at the trial level, the defendant failed to preserve his argument that he revoked the officers' implied license through his signage and that by ignoring this written revocation, the officers violated the Fourth Amendment.

State v. Degraphenreed, 261 N.C. App. 235 (2018). The court ruled that a car parked on the side of a public street opposite to the defendant's residence and outside the confines of the fence surrounding the residence was not within the residence's curtilage.

State v. Stanley, 259 N.C. App. 708, 717, 717–18 (2018). The knock and talk conducted by officers in this drug case violated the Fourth Amendment. After a confidential informant notified officers that he had purchased heroin from a person at an apartment, officers conducted three controlled drug buys at the apartment. On all three occasions the purchases were made at the back door of the apartment from an individual named Meager, who did not live there. Officers then obtained a warrant for Meager's arrest and approached the apartment to serve him. Upon arrival, they immediately walked down the driveway that led to the back of the apartment and knocked on the door. Events then transpired which led to, among other things, a patdown of the defendant and the discovery of controlled substances on the defendant's person. The defendant was arrested and charged with drug offenses. He filed a motion to suppress evidence obtained as a result of the officers' knock and talk. When it was denied, he pled guilty, reserving his right to appeal. On appeal, the court agreed that the knock and talk was unlawful. It held that "to pass constitutional muster, the officers were required to conduct the knock and talk by going to the front door, which they did not do. Rather than using the paved walkway that led directly to the unobstructed front door of the apartment, [they] walked along a gravel driveway into the backyard . . . to knock on the back door, which was not visible from the street. . . . [This] was . . . unreasonable." The court rejected the trial court's determination that the officers had an implied license to approach the back door because the confidential informant had purchased drugs there. The court stated that "the fact that the resident of a home may choose to allow certain individuals to use a back or side door does not mean that similar permission is deemed to have been given generally to members of the public." The court recognized that "unusual circumstances in some cases may allow officers to lawfully approach a door of the residence other than the front door in order to conduct a knock and talk." However, no such unusual circumstances were presented in this case.

State v. Huddy, 253 N.C. App. 148, 149, 154 (2017). The court ruled that an officer violated the defendant's Fourth Amendment rights by searching the curtilage of his home without a warrant. The officer saw a vehicle with its doors open at the back of a 150-yard driveway leading to the defendant's home. Concerned that the vehicle might be part of a break-in or home invasion, the officer drove down the driveway, ran the vehicle's tags, checked—but did not knock—on the front door, checked the windows and doors of the home for signs of forced entry, "cleared" the sides of the house, and then went through a closed gate in a chain-link fence enclosing the home's backyard and approached the storm door at the back of the house. As the officer approached the door, which was not visible from the street, he smelled marijuana, which led to the defendant's arrest for drug charges. The State relied on two exceptions to the warrant requirement in attempting to justify the officer's search of the curtilage: the knock and talk doctrine (under which law enforcement can do whatever a home's residents permit anyone else to do, i.e., walk up the home's front path, knock on the front door, wait for an answer, and leave if there is no answer) and the community caretaking doctrine (which permits law enforcement to take action in certain situations to protect the public even when they lack the suspicion required by the constitution to do so). The court found, however, that neither exception applied. First, the officer did more than merely knock and talk. Specifically, he ran a license plate not visible from the street, walked around the house examining windows and searching for signs of a break-in, and went to a rear door not visible from the street and located behind a closed gate. Likewise, the court ruled that the community caretaking doctrine did not support the officer's actions: "The presence of a vehicle in one's driveway with its doors open is not the sort of emergency that justifies the community caretaker exception." The court also noted that because the Fourth Amendment's protections "are at their very strongest within one's home," the public need justifying the community caretaking exception "must be particularly strong to justify a warrantless search of a home."

State v. Kirkman, 251 N.C. App. 274 (2016). In this drug case, the court ruled that an officer lawfully approached the front of the defendant's home and obtained information later used to procure a search warrant. Specifically, he heard a generator and noticed condensation and mold, factors that in his experience and training were consistent with the indoor cultivation of marijuana. The court stated that it is well-established that a law enforcement officer is permitted to approach a home's front door and that, if the officer is able to observe from that position conditions indicating illegal activity, it is "completely proper" to act upon information resulting from that observation.

Plain View (Sensory Perception) (page 297)
NORTH CAROLINA SUPREME COURT (page 299)

State v. Smith, 371 N.C. 469 (2018). The supreme court, per curiam and without an opinion, reversed the court of appeals, 255 N.C. App. 138 (2017), for the reasons stated in the dissenting opinion.

Three officers entered the defendant's apartment to execute misdemeanor arrest warrants (the officers knew that the defendant was on probation for an offense, although they did not know then if it was a felony or misdemeanor). While two of the officers made the in-home arrest, the third conducted a protective sweep of the defendant's apartment. A shotgun was leaning against the wall in the entry of the defendant's bedroom. The bedroom door was open, and the shotgun was visible, in plain view, from the hallway. The officer walked past the shotgun when checking the defendant's bedroom to confirm that no other occupants were present. After completing the sweep, the officer secured the shotgun in order to have it in police control and also to check to see if it was stolen. The officer located the serial number on the shotgun and called it into the police department, which reported that the gun was stolen. The officer then seized the weapon.

The defendant moved to suppress the shotgun, arguing that (1) the officer lacked authority to conduct a protective sweep and (2) the seizure could not be justified under the plain view doctrine. The trial court denied the defendant's motion to suppress. After determining that the protective sweep was proper (all three judges agreed on this issue) because the rooms in the apartment all adjoined the place of arrest and were locations from which an attack could be immediately launched (see *Maryland v. Buie*, 494 U.S. 325 (1990)), the court of appeals considered the seizure of the shotgun. Over a dissent, the court then ruled that the plain view doctrine could not justify seizure of the shotgun. The dissenting opinion, which was adopted by the supreme court, disagreed. It stated that the officers knew that the defendant had been placed on probation. A regular condition of probation is a ban on possessing firearms. Thus, the defendant's firearm was contraband that was unlawful to possess. Thus, it was immediately apparent that the shotgun was contraband, and the plain view doctrine justified its warrantless seizure.

NORTH CAROLINA COURT OF APPEALS (page 301)

State v. Johnson, ___ N.C. App. ___, 837 S.E.2d 179 (2019). An officer stopped at a gas station for a cup of coffee, and on his way inside he noticed the defendant standing outside the gas station, talking loudly and using abusive language on his cell phone. The clerk inside told the officer that she thought the defendant was bothering other customers. The officer called for backup and approached the defendant, and a second officer arrived. The first officer then asked the defendant to end his conversation. The defendant complied "after some delay," but then began shifting from foot to foot and looking from side to side. His nervous behavior made the officer concerned that he might have a weapon, so he asked the defendant if he could pat him down. The defendant hesitated, but then consented. While conducting the pat-down, the officer felt a soft, rubbery wad in the defendant's pocket that the officer immediately believed to be narcotics packaged in plastic baggies. After completing the pat-down, the officer manipulated the rubbery wad again, ensuring that it was what he believed it to be, and then reached into the defendant's pocket and withdrew the object. The wad was made up of plastic baggie corners containing a white powdery substance that looked like cocaine and a tube of Orajel. The defendant stated that the substance was baking soda, which he mixed with Orajel to fool buyers into thinking it was cocaine. Field and lab testing confirmed the defendant's statements. The defendant was charged with possession with intent to sell and deliver a counterfeit controlled substance. The trial court denied the defendant's motion to suppress the fruits of the search on the grounds that he was illegally detained, he did not consent to the search, and the search exceeded the scope of a permissible pat-down. The defendant pled guilty and appealed.

The court affirmed the trial court's ruling denying the motion. The defendant was not seized by the officers, who initially told him he should finish his conversation elsewhere. It was only when the defendant hesitated and began acting nervous that the first officer on the scene became concerned that the defendant might be armed, and the defendant then consented to be searched for weapons. The counterfeit drugs discovered during that weapons search were admissible under the "plain feel" doctrine. Even before he manipulated the object a second time or removed it from the defendant's pocket, the officer testified that based on his years of experience in narcotics investigations, it was "immediately apparent" to him that the object would be drugs in plastic packaging. After reviewing several cases on the plain feel doctrine, the court explained that the standard to be applied is analogous to the probable cause standard. In this case, the officer's training and experience in narcotics investigations, the circumstances surrounding the defendant's nervous behavior, and the readily apparent nature of the item in the defendant's pocket established that the officer's subsequent manipulation of the objects and search of the defendant's pocket for confirmation were therefore supported by probable cause.

Historical Cell-Site Information (page 308)

UNITED STATES SUPREME COURT (page 308)

Carpenter v. United States, 585 U.S. ___, ___, ___, 138 S. Ct. 2206, 2219, 2220 (2018). The court ruled that when the government accessed many days' worth of historical cell-site location information (CSLI) from a robbery suspect's wireless carriers, it invaded his "reasonable expectation of privacy in the whole of his physical movements," and thereby conducted a search under the Fourth Amendment. The Court stated that as a general rule, investigators must obtain a warrant supported by probable cause before they can acquire such records, unless an exception to the warrant requirement, such as exigency, is present. This effectively overrules prior North Carolina precedent and prohibits officers from using "reasonable grounds" court orders under 18 U.S.C. § 2703(d) to obtain long-term historical CSLI. *Carpenter* does not, however, address all the legal issues concerning cell phones and location information. For example, the majority expressly declined to opine about the Fourth Amendment status of "real-time CSLI or 'tower dumps' " and left open the possibility that obtaining only short-term historical CSLI would not be a search. For a detailed discussion of *Carpenter*, see Jeff Welty, *Supreme Court Rules that Obtaining Cell Site Location Information Is a Search*, UNC SCH. OF GOV'T: N.C. CRIM. L. BLOG (June 25, 2018), https://nccriminallaw.sog.unc.edu/9411-2/.

NORTH CAROLINA COURT OF APPEALS (page 308)

State v. Gore, ___ N.C. App. ___, 846 S.E.2d 295, 297, 298 (2020) (footnote omitted). The defendant pled guilty to manslaughter and armed robbery while preserving his right to appeal the denial of his motion to suppress historical cell-site location information (CSLI) obtained by the State without a search warrant. Evidence at the suppression hearing showed that police responded to a homicide and learned that a white Altima was seen leaving the scene. Officers soon located and boxed in the car, but the driver fled on foot and discarded a bloody handgun as he ran. Inside the car officers found drugs, a gun, and a blood-covered cell phone belonging to the defendant. Officers applied for a court order to obtain the records of the phone, including five days of CSLI from around the time of the homicide. The application was sworn under oath and supported by affidavit, and the order was issued based on a finding of probable cause. The phone records revealed that the defendant was in the area of the shooting when it occurred and was near the location of the white Altima when it was abandoned. The defendant moved to suppress the records because they were not obtained pursuant to a search warrant based on probable cause, in violation of his state and federal constitutional rights. The trial court denied the motion, finding that the court order in this case was the equivalent of a search warrant supported by probable cause. The court of appeals affirmed the trial court's ruling.

The court first addressed the defendant's federal constitutional claim. Citing *Carpenter v. United States*, 585 U.S. ___, 138 S. Ct. 2206 (2018), discussed immediately above, the court agreed that obtaining historical CSLI constituted a search, which requires a warrant supported by probable cause. A court order issued pursuant to the Stored Communications Act (SCA) based only on "reasonable grounds" to believe the records would be "relevant and material" to the investigation would not satisfy that standard. However, the order in this case was obtained two years before *Carpenter* was decided, and it was issued in compliance with the law at that time. Therefore, as in *Carpenter*, "even assuming law enforcement did conduct a warrantless search in violation of defendant's Fourth Amendment rights, the federal good-faith exception to the exclusionary rule would apply." (*See United States v. Leon*, 468 U.S. 897, 918 (1984) ("provid[ing] an exception . . . when 'officers acted in the objectively reasonable belief that their conduct did not violate the Fourth Amendment.' "))

Turning to the state constitutional claim, and noting that the state right at issue must be interpreted at least as broadly as the federal right, the court ruled that "a warrantless search of historical CSLI constitutes an unreasonable search in violation of a defendant's rights under the North Carolina Constitution as well." But after reviewing the statutory requirements for a search warrant and the probable cause standard, the court concluded that the order in this case did satisfy the search warrant requirement. First, although it was denominated a court order rather than a search warrant, it nevertheless contained all of the information required in a search warrant, such as the applicant's name, sworn allegations of fact to support the applicant's belief, and a request to produce the records. Second, although a court order issued under the SCA is only required to meet a "reasonable grounds" standard akin to reasonable suspicion, the order in this case was actually based upon a finding that there was *"Probable Cause* that the information sought is relevant and material to an ongoing criminal investigation, involving a First Degree Murder." The court stated that the finding of probable cause was a significant distinction that compelled a different outcome than that of *Carpenter*. Accordingly, because the trial court determined that there was probable cause to search the defendant's historical CSLI, the requirements for a warrant were met and the defendant's constitutional rights were not violated.

Search and Seizure by Valid Consent (page 316)

Voluntariness (page 316)

Generally (page 316)

NORTH CAROLINA COURT OF APPEALS (page 319)

State v. Bartlett, 260 N.C. App. 579 (2018). The court ruled that the trial court properly denied the defendant's motion to suppress heroin discovered following a search of the defendant during a traffic stop. A tactical narcotics officer noticed a Lincoln sedan weaving in and out of heavy traffic at high speeds, nearly causing multiple collisions. The vehicle pulled into a Sonic Drive-In parking lot next to an unoccupied Honda. The defendant, a passenger in the Lincoln, exited the vehicle, approached the Honda, and placed his hand inside the passenger window of that vehicle. The driver of the Honda appeared and spoke with the defendant briefly. The defendant then returned to the Lincoln and the vehicle drove away. No one in the Lincoln had ordered any food. Based on his experience, the officer concluded that the defendant had participated in a drug transaction. Other officers then saw the Lincoln go to a gas station. A second officer radioed that the vehicle continued to be driven in a careless and reckless manner, at approximately 15 m.p.h. over the speed limit. After the vehicle left the gas station, the first officer stopped it for reckless driving and speeding. Four other officers participated in the stop; all five officers were in uniform. The first officer approached the passenger side of the vehicle, while two others approached the driver's side. The officer approaching the passenger side saw the defendant reach towards the floorboard. Because he did not know whether the defendant had a weapon or was trying to conceal contraband, the officer asked the defendant to show him his hands. The defendant raised his hands, which were daubed in a light pink substance that the defendant stated was fabric softener. The officer ordered the defendant out of the vehicle and asked whether he was attempting to conceal something. The defendant denied doing so. The officer testified that when he asked for the defendant's consent to search his person the defendant gave consent saying, "go ahead." The defendant testified that he never consented to a search. When the officer proceeded to pat down the defendant, he noticed a larger than normal bulge near the groin area that was not consistent with "male parts." The officer then detained the defendant in handcuffs, believing that he had contraband on his person. The officer asked the defendant if he had anything inside of his underwear and the defendant said that he did. The officer asked the defendant if he would retrieve the item and the defendant said that he would. The officer removed the handcuffs and the defendant reached into his pants and produced a plastic bag containing heroin. He was then placed under arrest.

The court first found that the defendant consented to the search, rejecting the defendant's argument that his consent was not voluntary given the coercive environment fostered by the police. The defendant argued that his race is highly relevant to the determination of whether he voluntarily consented to the search because people of color will view a "request" to search by the police as an inherently coercive command, and he cited various studies in support of this claim. The court agreed that the defendant's race may be a relevant factor in considering whether consent was voluntary. It found, however, that aside from the studies presented by the defendant, the record was devoid of any indication that the defendant's consent in this case was involuntary. To the contrary, the circumstances showed that the defendant's consent was freely and intelligently made. Although multiple officers were present, only the first officer interacted with the defendant. When the officer approached the vehicle he asked the defendant whether he had anything illegal and the defendant said that he did not. The officer then asked if he could search the defendant's person, to which the defendant responded, "go ahead." No other conversation occurred. There is no evidence that the defendant was unaware of his ability to refuse the request or that he feared retribution had he done so. There is no indication that the officer made threats, used harsh language, or raised his voice. There is no evidence of any physical contact with the defendant. Additionally, the officers' firearms remained holstered throughout the encounter.

The court next rejected the defendant's argument that the scope of his consent to search his person did not include a frisk of his private parts and that, lacking probable cause or exigent circumstances to justify such a search, the pat-down of his groin area was unconstitutional. The court concluded that because the defendant's consent encompassed the sort of limited frisk that was performed, neither probable cause nor exigency was required to justify the search. The pat-down of the defendant's groin area was within the bounds of what a reasonable person would have expected the search to include. The officer limited his pat-down to the outer layer of the defendant's clothing. He did not reach into the defendant's pants to search his undergarments or directly touch his groin area. Nothing about the search involved the exposure of the defendant's private parts to the officer or to the public. And there is no evidence that the groin pat-down was conducted in an unreasonably offensive manner. Thus, the court concluded that a reasonable person in the defendant's position would have understood his consent to include the sort of limited outer pat-down that was performed here.

Finally, the court rejected the defendant's argument that the officer's continued detention of him after searching his groin area was not justified by the plain feel doctrine. During the pat-down the officer felt a bulge that he determined was not consistent with male body parts and was obviously contraband. When coupled with the totality of the circumstances already observed by the officer, this discovery amounted to reasonable suspicion justifying further detention of the defendant to question him about the contents of his clothing.

State v. Parker, 256 N.C. App. 319 (2017). The court ruled that the defendant's consent to search his person was not voluntary when it was given during a period of unlawful detention. Believing that a confrontation between the defendant and a woman was going to escalate into a fight after observing the two yelling at each other in a driveway, officers approached and asked for the defendant's identification. In the process of de-escalating the situation, an officer checked the defendant's record and verified that he had no pending warrants. Without returning his identification, the officer asked for and received the defendant's consent to search his person. The court determined that under these circumstances the defendant's consent was not given voluntarily, reasoning that the officers unlawfully detained the defendant by retaining his identification after they had satisfied the purpose of the initial detention.

State v. Cobb, 248 N.C. App. 687 (2016). In this drug case, the court held that the defendant's consent to search his room in a rooming house was voluntarily given. The court rejected the defendant's argument that he was in custody when consent was given. There was no evidence that the defendant's movements were limited by the officers during the encounter. Also, the officers did not supervise the defendant while they were in the home; rather, they simply followed the defendant to his room after he gave consent to search.

Scope of the Search (page 324)
NORTH CAROLINA COURT OF APPEALS (page 325)

State v. Bullock, 258 N.C. App. 72 (2018). [This case was decided after remand from the North Carolina Supreme Court, 370 N.C. 256 (2017).] During a traffic stop, the defendant consented to a search of his vehicle but not to a search of his personal belongings in it, a bag and two hoodies. After searching the vehicle, the officer's K-9—which had failed to alert to the vehicle—alerted to the presence of narcotics in the defendant's bag, which had been removed from the vehicle before the search began. The court ruled that the scope of the officer's search of the vehicle did not exceed the scope of the defendant's consent. Furthermore, the defendant did not revoke consent to search his vehicle. Although the defendant asked the officer what would happen if he revoked his consent, the defendant never revoked consent to search the vehicle, even after the officer explained that he needed to wait for a second officer to arrive to conduct the search.

Search and Seizure of Evidence with Probable Cause, Reasonable Suspicion, or Other Justification (page 336)

Vehicles, Including Containers within Vehicles (page 336)

Generally (page 336)

UNITED STATES SUPREME COURT (page 336)

Collins v. Virginia, 584 U.S. ___, ___, ___, ___, ___, 138 S. Ct. 1663, 1669, 1671, 1672, 1675 (2018). The Court ruled that the automobile exception to the Fourth Amendment does not permit an officer, uninvited and without a warrant, to enter the curtilage of a home to search a vehicle parked there. In this case, an officer saw the driver of an orange and black motorcycle with an extended frame commit a traffic infraction. The driver eluded the officer's attempt to stop the motorcycle. A few weeks later, another officer saw a similar motorcycle traveling well over the speed limit, but the driver got away from him, too. The officers compared notes and determined that the two incidents involved the same motorcyclist and that the motorcycle likely was stolen and in the possession of Ryan Collins. After discovering photographs on Collins's Facebook page showing an orange and black motorcycle parked at the top of the driveway of a house, one of the officers tracked down the address of the house, drove there, and parked on the street. It was later established that Collins's girlfriend lived in the house and that Collins stayed there a few nights per week. From the street, the officer saw what appeared to be the motorcycle in question. The officer, who did not have a warrant, walked towards the house. He stopped to take a photograph of the covered motorcycle from the sidewalk and then walked onto the residential property and up to the top of the driveway where the motorcycle was parked. He removed the tarp, revealing a motorcycle that looked like the one from the speeding incident. He ran a search of the license plate and vehicle identification numbers, which confirmed that the motorcycle was stolen. The officer photographed the uncovered motorcycle, put the tarp back on, left the property, and returned to his car to wait for the defendant. The defendant was ultimately arrested, and he unsuccessfully sought in Virginia trial and appellate courts to suppress the evidence the officer obtained as a result of the warrantless search of the motorcycle. The United States Supreme Court granted certiorari and reversed. The Court characterized the case as arising "at the intersection of two components of the Court's Fourth Amendment jurisprudence: the automobile exception to the warrant requirement and the protection extended to the curtilage of a home." After reviewing the law on these doctrines, the Court turned to whether the location in question is curtilage. It noted that according to photographs in the record, the driveway runs alongside the front lawn and up a few yards past the front perimeter of the house. The top portion of the driveway that sits behind the front perimeter of the house is enclosed on two sides by a brick wall about the height of a car and on a third side by the house. A side door provides direct access between this partially enclosed section of the driveway and the house. A visitor endeavoring to reach the front door would have to walk partway up the driveway but would turn off before entering the enclosure and instead proceed up a set of steps leading to the front porch. When the officer searched the motorcycle, it was parked inside this partially enclosed top portion of the driveway that abuts the house. The Court concluded that the driveway was properly considered curtilage. The Court continued, noting that by physically intruding on the curtilage, the officer not only invaded the defendant's Fourth Amendment interest in the item searched—the motorcycle—but also his interest in the curtilage of the home at which he was a guest. Finding the case an "easy" one, the Court concluded that the automobile exception did not justify an invasion of the curtilage. It clarified that "the scope of the automobile exception extends no further than the automobile itself." The Court rejected Virginia's request that it expand the scope of the automobile exception to permit police to invade any space outside an automobile even if the Fourth Amendment protects that space. It continued:

> Just as an officer must have a lawful right of access to any contraband he discovers in plain view in order to seize it without a warrant, and just as an officer must have a lawful right of access in order to arrest a person in his home, so, too, an officer must have a lawful right of access to a vehicle in

order to search it pursuant to the automobile exception. The automobile exception does not afford the necessary lawful right of access to search a vehicle parked within a home or its curtilage because it does not justify an intrusion on a person's separate and substantial Fourth Amendment interest in his home and curtilage.

The Court summed up that "the automobile exception does not permit an officer without a warrant to enter a home or its curtilage in order to search a vehicle therein." It left for resolution on remand whether the officer's warrantless intrusion on the curtilage may have been reasonable on a different basis, such as the exigent circumstances exception to the warrant requirement.

NORTH CAROLINA COURT OF APPEALS (page 339)

State v. Burton, 251 N.C. App. 600 (2017). The court rejected the defendant's claim that counsel was ineffective by failing to object to the admission of cocaine found during an officer's warrantless search of the defendant's vehicle; the court rejected the defendant's argument that the State was required to prove that the defendant's car was "readily mobile" in order for the automobile exception to the warrant requirement to apply. An officer searched the vehicle after smelling a strong odor of marijuana and seeing an individual sitting in the passenger seat with marijuana on his lap. The cocaine was found during a subsequent search of the vehicle. The vehicle was parked on the street when the search occurred and no evidence suggested it was incapable of movement.

Probable Cause to Search a Person (page 346)
NORTH CAROLINA COURT OF APPEALS (page 347)

State v. Pigford, 248 N.C. App. 797 (2016). The court ruled that the odor of marijuana emanating from inside a vehicle stopped at a checkpoint did not provide an officer with probable cause to conduct an immediate warrantless search of the driver. The defendant was driving the stopped vehicle, while a passenger sat in the front seat. The officer was unable to establish the exact location of the odor but determined that it was coming from inside the vehicle. Upon smelling the odor, the officer ordered the defendant out of the vehicle and searched him, finding cocaine and other items. On appeal the defendant argued that although the officer smelled marijuana emanating from the vehicle, there was no evidence that the odor was attributable to the defendant personally. While the officer had probable cause to search the vehicle, that does not necessarily justify the search of a passenger. The State offered no evidence that the marijuana odor was attributable to the defendant. The court stated that while the the officer might have had probable cause to search the vehicle, he did not have probable cause to search the defendant.

Warrantless Entry with Exigent Circumstances to Search a Place for Evidence or Weapons (page 348)
NORTH CAROLINA COURT OF APPEALS (page 349)

State v. Marrero, 248 N.C. App. 787, 793 (2016). The court ruled that the trial court properly denied a motion to suppress when the defendant was not illegally seized during a knock and talk, and exigent circumstances justified the officers' warrantless entry into the defendant's home. The court rejected the defendant's argument that he was illegally seized during a knock and talk because he was coerced into opening his front door. The officers knocked on the defendant's front door a few times and stated that they were with the police only once during the two to three minutes it took the defendant to answer the door. There was no evidence that the defendant was aware of the officers' presence before he opened the door. Blue lights from nearby police cars were not visible to the defendant and no takedown lights were used. The officers did not try to open the door themselves or demand that it be opened. The court concluded: "[T]he officers . . . did not act in a physically or verbally threatening manner" and no seizure of the defendant occurred during the knock and talk. Furthermore, exigent circumstances supported the officers' warrantless entry into the defendant's home. Officers arrived at the defendant's residence because of an informant's tip that armed suspects were going to rob a marijuana plantation located inside the house. When the officers arrived for the knock and talk, they did not know whether the robbery had occurred, was in progress, or was imminent. As soon as the defendant opened his door, an officer smelled a strong odor of marijuana. Based on that odor and the defendant's inability to understand English, the officers entered the defendant's home and secured it in preparation for obtaining a search warrant. On these facts, the trial court did not err in concluding that exigent circumstances warranted a protective sweep for officer safety and to ensure that neither the defendant nor others would destroy evidence.

Search and Seizure of Evidence from a Person's Body (page 358)
UNITED STATES SUPREME COURT (page 358)

Mitchell v. Wisconsin, 588 U.S. ___, 139 S. Ct. 2525 (2019). The defendant appealed from his impaired driving conviction and asserted that the State violated the Fourth Amendment by withdrawing his blood without a search warrant while he was unconscious following his arrest for impaired driving. A Wisconsin state statute permits such blood draws. The Wisconsin Supreme Court affirmed the petitioner's convictions, though no single opinion from that court commanded a majority, and the United States Supreme Court granted certiorari to decide whether a statute authorizing a blood draw from an unconscious motorist provides an exception to the Fourth Amendment warrant requirement.

Justice Alito, joined by Chief Justice Roberts, Justice Breyer, and Justice Kavanaugh, announced the judgment of the court and wrote the plurality opinion, which is the binding holding for lower courts. *See Marks v. United States,* 430 U.S. 188 (1977) (when a divided Court decides a case and no single rationale has the assent of at least five Justices, the Court's holding is the position taken by those members who concurred in the judgment on the narrowest ground). Justice Thomas joined the judgment but wrote a separate opinion that supported a broader ground than the plurality opinion.

The plurality opinion noted that the Court's opinions approving the general concept of implied consent laws did not rest on the idea that such laws create actual consent to the searches they authorize, but instead they approved defining elements of such statutory schemes after evaluating constitutional claims in light of laws developed over the years to combat impaired driving. The plurality stated that the Court had previously determined that an officer may withdraw blood from an impaired driving suspect without a warrant if the facts of a particular case establish exigent circumstances. *See Missouri* v. *McNeely,* 569 U.S. 141 (2013); *Schmerber* v. *California,* 384 U.S. 757 (1966).

While the natural dissipation of alcohol is insufficient by itself to create per se exigency in impaired driving cases, exigent circumstances may exist when the natural metabolic process is combined with other pressing law enforcement duties (such as the need to address issues resulting from a car accident) such that the further delay necessitated by a search warrant application risks the destruction of evidence. The plurality reasoned that in impaired driving cases involving unconscious drivers, the need for a blood test is compelling and the officer's duty to attend to more pressing needs involving health or safety (such as the need to transport an unconscious suspect to a hospital for treatment) may leave the officer with no time to obtain a search warrant. Thus, the plurality determined that when an officer has probable cause to believe that a person has committed an impaired driving offense and the person's unconsciousness or stupor requires the person to be taken to the hospital before a breath test may be performed, the State may "almost always" order a warrantless blood test to measure the driver's blood alcohol concentration without violating the Fourth Amendment. The plurality did not rule out that in an unusual case, a defendant could show that his or her blood would not have been withdrawn had the State not sought blood alcohol concentration information and that a warrant application would not have interfered with other pressing needs or duties. The plurality remanded the case because the petitioner did not have an opportunity to make such a showing.

Justice Thomas concurred in the judgment only, writing separately to advocate for overruling *McNeely* in favor of a rule that the dissipation of alcohol creates an exigency that excuses the need for a warrant in every impaired driving case.

[*Author's note*: The Fourth Amendment ruling in *State v. Romano*, 369 N.C. 678 (2017) (taking of blood in DWI investigation from unconscious defendant was not supported by exigent circumstances), decided before *Mitchell*, does not appear to comport with the *Mitchell* exigency test. *See* Shea Denning, *Supreme Court Announces New Exigency Test for Blood Draws from Unconscious DWI Suspects*, UNC SCH. OF GOV'T: N.C. CRIM. L. BLOG (July 9, 2019), https://www.sog.unc.edu/blogs/nc-criminal-law/supreme-court-announces-new-exigency-test-blood-draws-unconscious-dwi-suspects.]

NORTH CAROLINA COURT OF APPEALS (page 360)

State v. Burris, 253 N.C. App. 525 (2017). In this impaired driving case, the court ruled that the trial court properly denied the defendant's motion to suppress when exigent circumstances supported a warrantless blood draw. The defendant tested at .10 on a roadside breath sample test administered by Detective Hill, was arrested at 2:48 a.m., and then was transported to the police department, where he arrived eighteen minutes later. When the defendant refused to comply with further testing within two to three minutes after arriving at the police department, the detective decided to compel a blood test. The closest hospital was approximately four miles from the police department and eight miles from the magistrate's office. The detective read the defendant his rights regarding the blood draw at the hospital at 3:24 a.m. and waited for the defendant to finish making a phone call before starting the blood draw at 3:55 a.m. The detective testified that based on the information he had at the time, he thought that the defendant was close to a blood alcohol level of .08. The detective further indicated that he thought it would have taken an additional hour to an hour and a half to get a search warrant. The detective was the only officer on the scene and would have had to wait for another officer to arrive before he could travel to the magistrate to get the search warrant. The trial court's finding regarding the detective's reasonable belief that the delay would result in the dissipation of alcohol in the defendant's blood was supported by competent evidence. Thus, the trial court did not err in denying the defendant's suppression motion.

Probation or Parole Officer's Search of Home (page 364)

NORTH CAROLINA COURT OF APPEALS (page 364)

State v. Powell, 253 N.C. App. 590 (2017). The court ruled that because the State failed to meet its burden of demonstrating that a warrantless search was authorized by G.S. 15A-1343(b)(13), the trial court erred by denying the defendant's motion to suppress. The defendant was subject to the regular condition of probation under G.S. 15A-1343(b)(13). This provision requires that the probationer "[s]ubmit at reasonable times to warrantless searches by a probation officer of the probationer's person and of the probationer's vehicle and premises while the probationer is present, for purposes directly related to the probation supervision . . . ." Here, the search of the defendant's home occurred as part of an ongoing operation of a United States Marshal's Service task force. The court noted that while prior case law makes clear that the presence or participation of law enforcement officers does not, by itself, render a warrantless search under the statute unlawful, the State must meet its burden of satisfying the "purpose" element of the statute. The State failed to meet its burden here. To conclude otherwise would require the court to read the phrase "for purposes directly related to the probation supervision" out of the statute. The court emphasized that its opinion should not be read as diminishing the authority of probation officers to conduct warrantless searches of probationers' homes or to utilize the assistance of law enforcement officers in conducting such searches. Rather, it held that on the specific facts of this case, the State failed to meet its burden of demonstrating that the search was authorized under the statute.

Wiretapping, Eavesdropping, Digital Evidence, and Video Surveillance (page 365)
NORTH CAROLINA COURT OF APPEALS (page 366)

State v. Forte, 257 N.C. App. 505 (2018). The trial court issued an order authorizing law enforcement to access location information for the defendant's phone. The order was issued pursuant to the Stored Communications Act (SCA). The SCA requires only reasonable suspicion for issuance of an order for disclosure. The order was based on information provided by a known drug dealer informant, Oliver. The court found that there were "multiple indications of reliability" of Oliver's statements, including that he made substantial admissions against his penal interest. Also, Oliver provided a nickname, a general description of the defendant, background information from dealing with him previously, and current travel information regarding the defendant. Oliver spoke with the officer, and the two spoke more than once, adding to the reliability of his tip. These facts met the standard under the SCA. The court ruled that the defendant had not preserved any argument regarding whether the SCA's standard was unconstitutionally low.

Protective Searches (page 371)
Scope of Search Incident to Arrest (page 371)
Generally (page 371)
NORTH CAROLINA COURT OF APPEALS (page 374)

State v. Fuller, 257 N.C. App. 181 (2017). In this drug case, the court ruled that a search of the defendant's person was a proper search incident to arrest. An officer stopped the defendant's vehicle for driving with a revoked license and arrested the defendant. The officer then conducted a consent search of the vehicle that failed to locate any contraband, but a K-9 dog arrived and "hit" on the driver's seat cushion. When a second search uncovered no contraband or narcotics, the officer concluded that the narcotics must be on the defendant's person. The defendant was brought to the police department and was searched. The search involved lowering the defendant's pants and long johns to his knees. During the search the officer pulled out, but did not pull down, the defendant's underwear and observed the defendant's genitals and buttocks. Cocaine eventually was retrieved from a hidden area on the fly of the defendant's pants. The appellate court rejected the defendant's argument that the strip search could only have been conducted with probable cause and exigent circumstances, noting that standard applies only to roadside strip searches. Here, the search was conducted incident to the defendant's lawful arrest and inside a private interview room at a police facility. Furthermore, the scope of the search was reasonable. It was limited to the area of the defendant's body and clothing that would have come in contact with the cushion of the driver's seat where the dog alerted, and the defendant was searched inside a private interview room at the police station with only the defendant and two officers present. The officers did not remove the defendant's clothing above the waist. They did not fully remove his undergarments, nor did they touch his genitals or any body cavity. The court thus concluded that the place, manner, justification, and scope of the search of the defendant's person were reasonable.

Arrest of an Occupant of a Vehicle (page 375)
NORTH CAROLINA COURT OF APPEALS (page 376)

State v. Martinez, 251 N.C. App. 284 (2016). The court ruled that after the defendant's arrest for impaired driving, officers properly searched his vehicle as a search incident to arrest. Applying *Arizona v. Gant*, 556 U.S. 332 (2009), the court found that the officers had a reasonable basis to believe that evidence of impaired driving might be found in the vehicle. The defendant denied ownership, possession, and operation of the vehicle to the officer both verbally and by throwing the car keys under the vehicle. Based on the totality of the circumstances, including the strong odor of alcohol on the defendant, the defendant's efforts to hide the keys and refusal to unlock the vehicle, and the officers' training and experience with regard to impaired driving investigations, the trial court properly concluded that the officers reasonably believed the vehicle might have contained evidence of the offense. In the factual discussion, the court noted that one of the officers had testified that he had conducted between twenty and thirty impaired driving investigations; that at least 50 percent of those cases involved discovery of evidence associated with impaired driving inside the vehicle, such as open containers of alcohol; and that he had been trained to search a vehicle under these circumstances.

Protective Sweep of Premises (page 377)
NORTH CAROLINA SUPREME COURT (page 377)

State v. Smith, 371 N.C. 469 (2018). The court, per curiam and without an opinion, reversed the court of appeals, 255 N.C. App. 138 (2017), for the reasons stated in the dissenting opinion.

Three officers entered the defendant's apartment to execute misdemeanor arrest warrants (the officers knew that the defendant was on probation for an offense, although they did not know then if it was a felony or misdemeanor). While two of the officers made the in-home arrest, the third conducted a protective sweep of the defendant's apartment. A shotgun was leaning against the wall in the entry of the defendant's bedroom. The bedroom door was open, and the shotgun was visible in plain view from the hallway. The officer walked past the shotgun when checking the defendant's bedroom to confirm that no other occupants were present. After completing the sweep, the officer secured the shotgun in order to have it in police control and also to check to see if it was stolen. The officer located the serial number on the shotgun and called it into the police department, which reported that the gun was stolen. The officer then seized the weapon.

The defendant moved to suppress the shotgun, arguing that (1) the officer lacked authority to conduct a protective sweep and (2) the seizure could not be justified under the plain view doctrine. The trial court denied the defendant's motion to suppress. After determining that the protective sweep was proper (all three judges agreed on this issue) because the rooms in the apartment all adjoined the place of arrest and were locations from which an attack could be immediately launched (see *Maryland v. Buie,* 494 U.S. 325 (1990)), the court of appeals considered the seizure of the shotgun. Over a dissent, the court then held that the plain view doctrine could not justify seizure of the shotgun. The dissenting opinion, which was adopted by the supreme court, disagreed. It stated that the officers knew that the defendant had been placed on probation. A regular condition of probation is a ban on possessing firearms. Thus, the defendant's firearm was contraband that was unlawful to possess. Thus, it was immediately apparent that the shotgun was contraband, and the plain view doctrine justified its warrantless seizure.

Frisk (page 379)
Generally (page 379)
FEDERAL APPELLATE COURTS (page 399)

United States v. Robinson, 846 F.3d 694, 696 (4th Cir. 2017) (en banc). The Ranson, WV, police received an anonymous tip stating that not long ago a man in a parking lot that was widely known for drug-trafficking activity had loaded a firearm, concealed it in his pocket, and gotten into the passenger side of a blue-green Toyota Camry. After noticing that the occupants of a car meeting this description were not wearing seatbelts, police stopped the vehicle. Reasonably believing that the passenger in the Camry was armed, the police frisked him and discovered a firearm. They then arrested him for the possession of a firearm by a felon. The defendant moved to suppress the firearm, arguing that the officers lacked reasonable suspicion to believe that he was armed and dangerous, as they had no reason to believe that he was not a concealed-carry permit holder. The fourth circuit disagreed, concluding that when an officer makes a lawful traffic stop and has a reasonable suspicion that one of the occupants of the stopped vehicle is armed, the officer may frisk that individual for the officer's own protection and for the safety of anyone who may be on the scene. The court determined that a risk of danger sufficient to justify a frisk arises "from the combination of a forced police encounter and the presence of a weapon," even if the weapon is possessed legally. The court stated that for police officers, traffic stops are, in and of themselves, inherently dangerous. It also emphasized that determining whether a detainee is armed and dangerous does not require two separate inquiries; if a person is armed, by implication that person is dangerous. The court added that while the lawful stop of the defendant and the reasonable suspicion that he was armed justified the frisk in this case, the officers had knowledge of additional facts set out in its opinion that increased the level of their suspicion that he was dangerous.

Entering Premises for Public Safety Reasons (page 396)
NORTH CAROLINA COURT OF APPEALS (page 398)

State v. Huddy, 253 N.C. App. 148, 154 (2017). The court ruled that an officer violated the defendant's Fourth Amendment rights by searching the curtilage of his home without a warrant. The officer saw a vehicle with its doors open at the back of a 150-yard driveway leading to the defendant's home. Concerned that the vehicle might be part of a break-in or home invasion, the officer drove down the driveway, ran the vehicle's tags, checked the windows and doors of the home for signs of forced entry, "cleared" the sides of the house, and then went through a closed gate in a chain-link fence enclosing the home's backyard and approached the storm door at the back of the house. As the officer approached the door, which was not visible from the street, he smelled marijuana, which led to the defendant's arrest for drug charges. The court determined that this was not a knock and talk because the officer went to a rear door not visible from the street and located behind a closed gate. Likewise, the community caretaking doctrine (which permits law enforcement to take action in certain situations to protect the public even when they lack the suspicion required by the constitution to do so) did not support the officer's actions because a vehicle's doors may stand ajar for many reasons that are not suspicious. The court pointed out that the presence of a vehicle in a person's driveway with its doors open was not the type of emergency that justified the community caretaker exception to the warrant requirement. The court also noted that because the protections granted under the Fourth Amendment are considered to be at their strongest within a person's home, the public need justifying the community caretaking exception "must be particularly strong to justify a warrantless search of a home."

Chapter 4

Search Warrants, Administrative Inspection Warrants, and Nontestimonial Identification Orders

Footnote 1 (page 405)

The following sentence is to be added at the end this footnote. Although not binding on appellate or trial courts, the following cases are of some interest: (1) A concurring opinion in *State v. Gore*, ___ N.C. App. ___, 846 S.E.2d 295 (2020), concluded that the amendment to G.S. 15A-974 added by S.L. 2011-6, discussed earlier in this footnote, created a valid good-faith exception because the state constitution does not forbid the General Assembly from passing a law to allow a good-faith exception to the judicially adopted rule that evidence collected in violation of the constitution generally must be excluded and (2) the court of appeals in *State v. Foster*, 264 N.C. App. 135 (2019) (unpublished), noted in footnote 2 that the defendant argued that *State v. Carter*, 322 N.C. 709 (1988), stood for the proposition that there is no good-faith exception to the exclusionary rule under the North Carolina Constitution, but the language in *Carter* has been superseded by the amendment added to G.S. 15A-974 by S.L. 2011-6.

Part I: Search Warrants (page 406)

Introduction (page 406)
Consequences of an Unlawful Search or Seizure (page 406)
Exclusionary Rules (page 407)
North Carolina statutory exclusionary rule (page 408)
Footnote 20 (page 408)

Add to footnote 20 the following citation: *Cf.* State v. Downey, 249 N.C. App. 415 (2016) (holding that the statutory exclusionary rule did not apply in a case in which the defendant claimed that the inventory was vague and inaccurate, as no evidence was seized as a result of any fault regarding the inventory).

Description of the Property to Be Seized (page 413)

For a discussion of the requirement that the property to be seized be described with particularity, see Jeff Welty, *Particularly Describing the Evidence to Be Seized under a Search Warrant*, UNC Sch. of Gov't: N.C. Crim. L. Blog (Feb. 26, 2018), https://nccriminallaw.sog.unc.edu/particularly-describing-evidence-seized-search-warrant/.

Obscene Materials, Including Child Pornography (page 418)

A 2016 case has resolved two legal questions concerning search warrants for child pornography. First, it is now clear that an application for a search warrant in a child pornography case does *not* need to include a copy of the image or images in question in order to establish probable cause.[1] Second, it is also now settled that when an image possessed by a suspect can be matched to a known image of child pornography through its SHA-1 or "hash" value, that is sufficient to provide probable cause.[2] When a SHA-1 match is not possible, officers will often seek search warrants based on verbal descriptions of images viewed by an officer or another witness; in such a case, the description may need to be rather detailed and explicit to be sufficient.[3]

Description of the Premises, the Person to Be Searched, or the Vehicle (page 419)

The Premises (page 419)

Vehicles on the Premises (page 420)

In *State v. Lowe*,[4] the North Carolina Supreme Court ruled that a search warrant for a residence supported the search of a vehicle located within the curtilage of the home even though the vehicle (1) was not listed in the warrant and (2) did not belong to the occupant of the premises, as it was a rental vehicle in the possession of an overnight guest. The court stated that "[b]ecause the rental car was within the curtilage of the residence targeted by the search warrant, and because the rental car was a [place in which the object of the search, in this case drugs, could be located,] we conclude that the search of the rental car was authorized by the warrant."[5]

Statement of Facts Showing Probable Cause to Search (page 423)

Sources of Information to Establish Probable Cause (page 423)

Affiant's Use of Hearsay Information (page 425)

Information from confidential informants (page 426)

Informant's credibility or the reliability of the informant's information (page 427)

The evidence supporting an informant's reliability need not be overwhelming, as several relatively recent cases illustrate. First, in *State v. Jackson*,[6] the North Carolina Court of Appeals considered the following facts: Two officers, working on a drug investigation, performed a knock and talk at the home of a person who was not known to them. The officers told the resident that she was facing potential criminal charges for possessing marijuana. The resident then agreed to give the officers information about where she obtained the drugs.

---

1. State v. Gerard, 249 N.C. App. 500, 511 (2016) (so holding, and stating that "[i]ncluding copies of the images themselves would further perpetuate the very harm the statutes regarding child pornography were intended to prevent," i.e., the dissemination of inappropriate images).

2. *Id.* (noting that SHA1 or SHA-1 is an "algorithm" that is "like a fingerprint," which may be used to identify digital files, and stating that "[u]sing the SHA1 information to identify the known images of child pornography eliminated the need to attach copies of the images to the affidavit").

3. For a summary of the case law regarding verbal descriptions of images, see Jeff Welty, *Probable Cause and Child Pornography*, UNC SCH. OF GOV'T: N.C. CRIM. L. BLOG (Feb. 12, 2018), https://nccriminallaw.sog.unc.edu/probable-cause-child-pornography/.

4. 369 N.C. 360 (2016).

5. *Id.* at 367. For a longer discussion of *Lowe*, see Bob Farb, *North Carolina Supreme Court Upholds Search of Vehicle Located on Premises as Within Scope of Search Warrant*, UNC. SCH. OF GOV'T: N.C. CRIM. L. BLOG (Jan. 10, 2017), https://nccriminallaw.sog.unc.edu/north-carolina-supreme-court-upholds-search-vehicle-located-premises-within-scope-search-warrant/.

6. 249 N.C. App. 642, *aff'd*, 370 N.C. 337 (2017).

She told the officers she had purchased the marijuana from a named person (the defendant) at his residence two days earlier. She described the individual as well as his home and its location. The officers confirmed the accuracy of the suspect's name and the description and location of his home. They also learned that the suspect had previously been charged with possessing marijuana. Relying on this information plus the fact that they had received several citizen complaints about possible marijuana dealing at the suspect's residence over the past year, the officers sought and obtained a search warrant for his home. When they executed the warrant, they found marijuana and indoor growing equipment.

The court determined that the search warrant was supported by sufficient probable cause. Although the informant did not have a "track record" of providing reliable information, the court found that she was sufficiently reliable. The court emphasized that the informant had a face-to-face communication with the officers, during which they could assess her demeanor; this significantly increased the likelihood that she would be held accountable for information that later proved to be false. The court also found it significant that the informant had first-hand knowledge of the information she conveyed, that the police independently corroborated certain information she provided, and that the information was recent. Finally, the court stated that the information provided by the informant was likely reliable because it was against her penal interest. (However, although she admitted to criminal activity in purchasing and possessing marijuana, her motive in providing the information was apparently to reduce her criminal exposure rather than to come clean about her conduct.)[7]

The second relatively recent case is *State v. Brody*.[8] It addresses how extensive an informant's track record must be before the informant may be deemed reliable. The case arose out of a drug investigation in Charlotte. An officer applied for a search warrant for the defendant's home, stating that the officer had received information from "a confidential and reliable informant"[9] that the defendant was dealing drugs from his residence. Specifically, the informant claimed to have been in the defendant's home more than thirty times, including within the last forty-eight hours, and stated that he had seen evidence of drug dealing each time. Further, the affidavit supporting the warrant application indicated that the informant had "purchased cocaine from [the defendant] under the direct supervision of"[10] the officer, though the application did not detail the time, place, or circumstances of the purchase. The affidavit further stated that the officers had "known this informant for approximately two weeks"[11] and that the informant had "provided information on other persons involved in drug trafficking . . . which we have investigated independently."[12] The controlled buy, of course, strongly supported probable cause, but the court also commented on the reliability of the informant, stating that "[t]he fact that the affidavit did not describe the precise outcomes of the previous tips . . . did not preclude a determination that the [informant] was reliable."[13] The court stated that "[a]lthough a general averment that an informant is 'reliable'—taken alone—might raise questions as to the basis for such an assertion,"[14] the fact that the officer also referenced receiving information from the informant in the past "allows for a reasonable inference that such information demonstrated the [confidential informant's] reliability."[15]

Information from records (page 428)

A suspect's utility records may help establish probable cause by showing usage patterns consistent with criminal activity. For example, unusually high electricity consumption may be indicative of an indoor

---

7. For more information about *Jackson*, see Jeff Welty, *Drug Users, Drug Sellers, and Probable Cause*, UNC Sch. of Gov't: N.C. Crim. L. Blog (Oct. 11, 2016), https://nccriminallaw.sog.unc.edu/drug-users-drug-sellers-probable-cause/.

8. 251 N.C. App. 812 (2017).

9. *Id.* at 815.

10. *Id.*

11. *Id.*

12. *Id.*

13. *Id.* at 819.

14. *Id.*

15. *Id.*

marijuana growing operation using artificial lights. However, for this evidence to be meaningful, officers should provide context: "The weight given to power records increases when meaningful comparisons are made between a suspect's current electricity consumption and prior consumption, or between a suspect's consumption and that of nearby, similar properties."[16]

The Connection between a Crime, the Evidence to Be Seized, and the Place to Be Searched (page 430)

Several recent cases have addressed whether certain facts, clearly sufficient to establish probable cause that a crime had been committed, provided a sufficient nexus to a premises to support the search of that location. *State v. Allman*[17] is a case in which the North Carolina Supreme Court ultimately found that the facts showed a connection between a crime and the suspects' residence sufficient to support a search of the home. A deputy stopped and searched a car occupied by two half-brothers, finding marijuana and $1,600 in cash. Both occupants had prior drug arrests or convictions. One of them told the deputy that they lived together at an address in Castle Hayne, but when an officer later went to the residence, the men's mother answered the door and said that they lived at a different residence in Wilmington.

The deputy obtained a search warrant for the Wilmington address based on (1) the contents of the brothers' vehicle, (2) the men's history, (3) the officer's experience that drug dealers often keep evidence of drug dealing at their homes, and (4) the false statement regarding the men's address. The case eventually reached the state supreme court, which ruled that there was probable cause to support the search warrant. *Allman* does not go so far as to hold that evidence that a person is involved in drug activity will *always* allow a search of the person's residence. However, in this case, the facts cited above, especially the officer's experience and the false statement about where the men lived, were sufficient to support the issuance of the warrant.[18]

On the other hand, *State v. Lewis*[19] is an example of a case in which officers did *not* present a sufficient nexus to a premises. Officers investigated a series of armed robberies. They determined that the robberies had been committed by Robert Lewis and that he had used a Kia Optima or a Nissan Titan in each crime. An officer determined that Lewis lived at 7085 Laurinburg Road, went there, and saw an Optima and a Titan parked at the home. When Lewis came out of the residence, the officer arrested him. Another officer then applied for a search warrant for the vehicles and the residence. The North Carolina Supreme Court noted that the warrant to search the residence—though much of the information in the supporting affidavit linked the defendant to the robberies—failed to (1) disclose that the defendant lived at the residence; (2) contain any other information linking the defendant to that address; (3) describe the circumstances surrounding his arrest at that address, including that a Kia was parked at the residence at the time of arrest; or (4) mention the detective's interactions with the defendant or his stepfather, the latter having confirmed that the defendant lived at the residence. Absent information linking the defendant to the residence, the court ruled that the magistrate lacked probable cause to issue a warrant to search it, and so the defendant's motion to suppress should have been granted.

---

16. State v. Benters, 367 N.C. 660, 670, 671 (2014) (finding no probable cause despite an officer's statement that "the kilowatt usage hours [at the target residence] are indicative of a marijuana grow operation based on the extreme high and low kilowatt usage" because "the absence of any comparative analysis severely limits the potentially significant value of defendant's utility records").

17. 369 N.C. 292 (2016).

18. For further discussion of *Allman*, see Bob Farb, *North Carolina Supreme Court Upholds a Magistrate's Finding of Probable Cause to Issue Search Warrant to Search Home for Drugs*, UNC Sch. of Gov't: N.C. Crim. L. Blog (Jan. 24, 2017), https://nccriminallaw.sog.unc.edu/north-carolina-supreme-court-upholds-magistrates-finding-probable-cause-issue-search-warrant-search-home-drugs/.

19. 372 N.C. 576 (2019).

A related issue is the extent to which probable cause to believe a person committed a crime provides probable cause to search the person's cell phone for evidence of the crime. See the blog post cited in the accompanying footnote.[20]

Execution and Return of the Search Warrant (page 437)

Scope of the Search (page 440)

Vehicles on the Premises (page 442)

In *State v. Lowe*,[21] the North Carolina Supreme Court ruled that a search warrant for a residence supported the search of a vehicle located within the curtilage of the home even though the vehicle (1) was not listed in the warrant and (2) did not belong to the occupant of the premises, as it was a rental vehicle in the possession of an overnight guest. The court stated that "[b]ecause the rental car was within the curtilage of the residence targeted by the search warrant, and because the rental car was a [place in which the object of the search, in this case drugs, could be located,] we conclude that the search of the rental car was authorized by the warrant."[22]

People on the Premises (page 442)

Nonpublic Place (page 442)

Detaining and frisking (page 442)

In *State v. Wilson*, 371 N.C. 920 (2018), the North Carolina Supreme Court ruled that *Michigan v. Summers*, 452 U.S. 692 (1981), justified a seizure of the defendant when he posed a real threat to the safe and efficient completion of a search warrant execution, and that the later search of the defendant was supported by individualized suspicion. A SWAT team was sweeping a house so that the police could execute a search warrant. Several officers were positioned around the house to create a perimeter securing the scene. The defendant penetrated the SWAT perimeter, stating that he was going to get his moped. In so doing, he passed Officer Christian, who was stationed at the perimeter near the street. The defendant then kept going, moving up the driveway and towards the house to be searched. Officer Ayers, who was stationed near the house, confronted the defendant. After a brief interaction, Officer Ayers searched the defendant based on his suspicion that the defendant was armed. Officer Ayers found a firearm in the defendant's pocket. The defendant, who had previously been convicted of a felony, was arrested and charged with being a felon in possession of a firearm. He unsuccessfully moved to suppress evidence of the firearm at trial and was convicted.

The court of appeals ruled that the search was invalid because the trial court's order did not show that the search was supported by reasonable suspicion. The state supreme court reversed, holding that the rule in *Michigan v. Summers* justified the seizure here because the defendant, who passed one officer, stated that he was going to get his moped. He continued towards the premises being searched and posed a real threat to the safe and efficient completion of the search. The court interpreted the *Summers* rule to mean that a warrant to search for contraband founded on probable cause implicitly carries with it the limited authority to detain occupants who are within the immediate vicinity of the premises to be searched and who are present during the execution of a search warrant. Applying this rule, the court determined that a person is an occupant for the purposes of the *Summers* rule if he or she poses a real threat to the safe and efficient execution of a search warrant. Here, the defendant posed such a threat. The court reasoned that he approached the house

---

20. Jeff Welty, *Probable Cause and Search Warrants for Cell Phones*, UNC Sch. of Gov't: N.C. Crim. L. Blog (Oct. 3, 2016), https://nccriminallaw.sog.unc.edu/probable-cause-search-warrants-cell-phones/.

21. 369 N.C. 360 (2016).

22. *Id*. at 367. For a longer discussion of *Lowe*, see Farb, *North Carolina Supreme Court Upholds Search of Vehicle Located on Premises as Within Scope of Search Warrant*, *supra* note 5.

being swept, announced his intent to retrieve his moped from the premises, and appeared to be armed. It was obvious that the defendant posed a threat to the safe completion of the search.

Because the *Summers* rule only justifies detentions incident to the execution of search warrants, the court went on to consider whether the later search of the defendant's person was justified. On this issue the court held that search of the defendant was supported by individualized suspicion and thus did not violate the Fourth Amendment.

Part II. Administrative Inspection Warrants (page 448)

Authority for Issuing Administrative Inspection Warrants (page 448)

In the 2016 legislative session, the General Assembly made minor revisions to the city (G.S. 160A-424) and county (G.S. 153A-364) inspection statutes discussed in the main text.[23] The revisions do not affect the discussion of legal principles in the main text.

Part III. Nontestimonial Identification Orders (page 459)

Application for the Order and Issuance of the Order; Adult and Juvenile Suspect Forms (page 461)

This section of the main text states that the adult forms should be used for "a person who is charged with a crime committed on or after his or her 16th birthday," as well as for a juvenile who has been charged as an adult or who has been transferred to adult court. Footnote 275 explains that age 16 is the cutoff because G.S. 7B-2103 governs nontestimonial identification orders for juveniles "alleged to be delinquent," which under then-existing law meant juveniles under age 16. However, the Juvenile Justice Reinvestment Act, S.L. 2017-57, Section 16D.4., raised the age of juvenile jurisdiction to 18 in most cases,[24] effective for offenses committed on or after December 1, 2019. Therefore, for those offenses committed after that date, the adult forms should be used only for a person age 18 and over or for a juvenile who has been charged as an adult (see the discussion in "Juvenile's Age" below) or who has been transferred to adult court.

The Nontestimonial Identification Procedure (page 462)

Add the following case in footnote 286: State v. Hoque, ___ N.C. App. ___, 837 S.E.2d 464 (2020) (when defendant for whom search warrant was issued for blood sample resisted hospital nurse's attempts to take sample, officers pinned defendant to a bed; court ruled that force was reasonable under Fourth Amendment).

---

23. *See* S.L. 2016-122.

24. Not included in "most cases," for example, are all G.S. Chapter 20 motor vehicle offenses committed by a person at age 16 or 17, which continue to be tried in adult court. *See* Jacquelyn Greene, *Raise the Age Tips and Resources for Law Enforcement*, UNC Sch. of Gov't: N.C. Crim. L. Blog (Nov. 26, 2019), https://nccriminallaw.sog.unc.edu/raise-the-age-tips-and-resources-for-law-enforcement/. The definition of the term *delinquent juvenile* in G.S. 7B-1501(7) includes "[a]ny juvenile who, while less than 18 years of age but at least 16 years of age, commits a crime or an infraction under State law or under an ordinance of local government, *excluding* all violations of the motor vehicle laws under Chapter 20 of the General Statutes" (emphasis added).

Juveniles and Nontestimonial Identification Procedures (page 464)

Footnote 303 (page 464)

The first sentence of the footnote's text should be revised and expanded into three sentences as follows: Under G.S. 7B-1604, a juvenile who is emancipated must be prosecuted as an adult. A juvenile must be prosecuted as an adult for any criminal offense the juvenile commits after a district or superior court conviction if either of the following applies: (1) the juvenile had previously been transferred to and convicted in superior court or (2) the juvenile has previously been convicted in either district or superior court for a felony or misdemeanor, but any violation of the motor vehicle laws punishable as a misdemeanor or infraction is not considered a conviction unless it was impaired driving or commercial impaired driving. Under the definition of *delinquent juvenile* in G.S. 7B-1501(7), a person 16- or 17-years-old must be prosecuted as an adult for a crime or an infraction that is a violation of the motor vehicle laws under G.S. Chapter 20.

Juvenile's Age (page 465)

The Juvenile Justice Reinvestment Act, S.L. 2017-57, Section 16D.4., raised the age of juvenile jurisdiction to 18 in most cases,[25] effective for offenses committed on or after December 1, 2019. This legislative change requires the use of the juvenile nontestimonial identification procedures in G.S. 7B-2103 *et seq.* for offenses committed at ages 16 and 17 that now fall under juvenile jurisdiction, rather than the adult nontestimonial identification procedures in G.S. 15A-271 *et seq.* Most offenses committed at ages 16 and 17 and on or after December 1, 2019, fall under juvenile jurisdiction with the following exceptions. A juvenile must be tried in adult court when (1) the juvenile has been emancipated;[26] (2) the juvenile at age 16 or 17 was charged with a violation of the motor vehicle laws of G.S. Chapter 20;[27] or (3) the juvenile commits a criminal offense after a district or superior court conviction and either of the following applies: (a) the juvenile had previously been transferred to and convicted in superior court or (b) the juvenile had previously been convicted in either district or superior court for a felony or misdemeanor, excluding any violation of motor vehicle laws punishable as a misdemeanor or infraction, unless the conviction was for impaired driving or commercial impaired driving.[28] In all of these circumstances the offense will not fall under juvenile jurisdiction, and the adult procedures therefore apply.[29]

Show-Up Identification Conducted Shortly after Crime without Nontestimonial Identification Order (page 465)

Despite G.S. 7B-2103 (generally requiring a nontestimonial identification order to conduct a nontestimonial identification procedure), an officer must photograph a juvenile suspect who is 10 years of age or older at the time and place of a show-up if the juvenile is reported to have committed a nondivertible offense under G.S. 7B-1701[30] or common law robbery. G.S. 15A-284.52(c1), enacted in 2019, also sets out duties concerning the retention or disposal of any photos and who may examine them and under what conditions.[31]

---

25. The contents of the immediately preceding footnote pertain here.

26. G.S. 7B-1604(a).

27. The definition of the term *delinquent juvenile* in G.S. 7B-1501(7) includes "[a]ny juvenile who, while less than 18 years of age but at least 16 years of age, commits a crime or an infraction under State law or under an ordinance of local government, *excluding* all violations of the motor vehicle laws under Chapter 20 of the General Statutes" (emphasis added).

28. G.S. 7B-1604(b).

29. See the first sentence of G.S. 7B-2103 ("nontestimonial identification procedures shall not be conducted on any juvenile without a court order . . . unless the juvenile has been charged as an adult or transferred to superior court for trial as an adult in which case procedures applicable to adults . . . shall apply").

30. The nondivertible offenses are murder, first-degree rape and sexual offense, second-degree rape and sexual offense, arson, any felony violation of Article 5 (Controlled Substances Act) of G.S. Chapter 90, first-degree burglary, crime against nature, and any felony that involves the willful infliction of serious bodily injury on another or that is committed with the use of a deadly weapon.

31. S.L. 2019-47, effective June 17, 2019.

Chapter 4 Appendix: Case Summaries

I. Search Warrants (page 475)

Probable Cause (page 475)

Generally (page 475)

NORTH CAROLINA SUPREME COURT (page 476)

State v. Lewis, 372 N.C. 576 (2019). On discretionary review of a consolidated appeal from two decisions of the court of appeals, 259 N.C. App. 366 (2018), and 259 N.C. App. 424 (2018) (unpublished), the supreme court affirmed in part and reversed in part.

A sheriff's deputy arrested Robert Lewis, the defendant, who had been recognized as the possible perpetrator of a string of bank robberies committed over two months. After arresting the defendant, the deputy observed in plain sight a BB&T money bag on the floor of a Kia Optima that matched the description of a vehicle reportedly used to flee the scene of one of the robberies. The deputy also spoke with the defendant's stepfather, who confirmed that the defendant lived at the residence. A detective prepared a search warrant application seeking permission to search the residence where the defendant was arrested, the Kia, and another vehicle reportedly used to flee a different robbery. The affidavit accompanying the search warrant application failed to list several pieces of information. It did not (1) disclose that the defendant lived at the residence; (2) contain any other information linking the defendant to that address; (3) describe the circumstances surrounding his arrest at that address, including that a Kia was parked at the residence then; or (4) mention the deputy's interactions with the defendant or his stepfather, who had confirmed that the defendant lived at the residence. Absent information linking the defendant to the residence, the court ruled that the magistrate lacked probable cause to issue a warrant to search it, and so the court affirmed the court of appeals' ruling that the defendant's motion to suppress evidence obtained from the search should have been granted. A magistrate nonetheless issued the warrant, which led to the seizure of more evidence linking the defendant to the robberies.

The defendant filed multiple motions to suppress, arguing that there was an insufficient connection between the items sought and the property to be searched, and that the search of the Kia was not permissible under the plain view doctrine. The trial court denied the motion. The court of appeals ruled that the detective's search warrant application was sufficient to establish probable cause to search the cars but insufficient to establish probable cause to search the dwelling because the supporting affidavit failed to state that the defendant resided there.

The supreme court noted that the warrant to search the residence—though much of the information in the supporting affidavit linked the defendant to the robberies—failed to set forth the circumstances of the defendant's arrest at this particular address, including how the detective who prepared the warrant initially obtained the address from officers in Johnston County, and how the defendant's stepfather had confirmed where the defendant resided. Absent information linking the defendant to the residence, the court ruled that the magistrate lacked probable cause to issue a warrant to search it, and so the court affirmed the court of appeals' ruling that the defendant's motion to suppress should have been granted. Concerning the search of the Kia, the court concluded that the limited information actually set out in the affidavit failed to establish probable cause for the search. As a result, the court reversed the portion of the court of appeals' decision concluding that there was probable cause and remanded the case for consideration of the trial judge's alternative finding that the vehicle search was valid under the plain view doctrine.

State v. Frederick, 371 N.C. 547 (2018). The supreme court affirmed per curiam and without an opinion the ruling of the court of appeals, 259 N.C. App. 165 (2018), that probable cause supported a search warrant. A detective sought a search warrant for the defendant's home. The affidavit in support of the warrant application stated that a "confidential source" had recently given the officer "information . . . regarding a [drug] dealer." The detective considered the source reliable, as he had previously provided accurate information. The detective and the source attempted to corroborate the information by conducting two controlled buys in the week before the warrant application was submitted. In both cases, the informant met with a "middle man," who was apparently unknown to the detective, and took him to the suspect's home. Officers watched the middle man enter the home and exit a few minutes later. The informant dropped the middle man off at his residence and then met with the detective. Each time, the informant had no drugs at the outset and had drugs at the end of the event. A magistrate issued a search warrant based on these transactions, and the court of appeals ruled that probable cause supported the issuance of the search warrant.

State v. Lowe, 369 N.C. 360 (2016). A search warrant authorizing a search of the premises where the defendant was arrested was supported by probable cause. The affidavit supporting the warrant stated that officers received an anonymous tip that Michael Turner was selling, using, and storing narcotics at his house; that Turner had a history of drug-related arrests; and that a detective discovered marijuana residue in the trash from Turner's residence, along with correspondence addressed to Turner. Under the totality of the circumstances, there was probable cause to search the home for controlled substances.

NORTH CAROLINA COURT OF APPEALS (page 479)

State v. Lenoir, 259 N.C. App. 857 (2018). The court held that an application for a search warrant contained insufficient details to support issuance of the warrant. When officers went to the defendant's home to conduct a knock and talk, the defendant's brother answered the door and invited them in. After an officer asked if anyone else was present, the brother said he was alone but gave consent for the officer to check a back bedroom. In the bedroom the officer saw a woman lying on a bed and a "glass smoke pipe" on a dresser. The officer applied for and was issued a search warrant for the residence. A search of the home revealed a shotgun in the back bedroom. After the defendant admitted that he owned the gun, he was charged with possession of a firearm by a felon. On review, the court observed that the affidavit supporting the warrant application stated that the officer saw a "smoke pipe used for methamphetamine" in the bedroom. The application did not mention the officer's training and experience, nor did the officer provide information explaining the basis for his belief that the pipe was being used to smoke methamphetamine as opposed to tobacco. The affidavit did not explain how the officer was qualified to distinguish between a pipe used for lawful versus unlawful purposes. And it did not purport to describe in any detail the appearance of the pipe or contain any indication as to whether it appeared to have been recently used. The affidavit further lacked any indication that information had been received connecting the defendant or his home to drugs. The court stated that "a pipe—standing alone—is neither contraband nor evidence of a crime." Because the affidavit was insufficient to establish probable cause for issuance of the warrant, the court ruled that the trial court erred in denying the defendant's motion to suppress the shotgun.

Timeliness or Staleness of Information (page 484)
NORTH CAROLINA COURT OF APPEALS (page 484)

State v. Winchester, 260 N.C. App. 418, 425 (2018) (citations omitted). The court upheld the validity of a warrant to search the defendant's vehicle, person, and residence. Based on recitations in the supporting affidavit of multiple trash pulls at the defendant's residence revealing drug-dealing evidence, the last occurring one week before the warrant application, the court found that this evidence was not stale. The court relied on statements from *State v. McCoy*, 100 N.C. App. 574, 577 (1990), that when an affidavit recites facts indicating protracted and continuous activity showing a course of conduct, the passage of time is a less significant factor. Quoting *McCoy*, the court stated that "[t]he continuity of the offense may be the most important factor in determining whether the probable cause is valid or stale."

State v. Teague, 259 N.C. App. 904 (2018). The court held that an application provided sufficient probable cause to support the issuance of a search warrant for the defendant's residence. The supporting affidavit indicated that after an officer received an anonymous tip that drugs were being sold at the defendant's residence, he conducted a "refuse investigation" at the premises, finding evidence of drug activity in the trash. The defendant asserted that this information was stale and could not properly support issuance of the warrant. The court noted that although the affidavit did not state when or over what period of time the tipster observed criminal activity at the residence, when the tipster relayed the information to the police, or the exact date the officer conducted the refuse search, the affidavit was based on more than just this information. Specifically, it included details regarding database searches indicating that the defendant had a waste and water utility account at the residence, that the defendant lived at the residence, that the officer was familiar with the residence and the defendant from his previous assignment as a patrol officer, and that the defendant had prior drug charges. To the extent that the information in the anonymous tip was stale, it was later corroborated by the refuse search in which the officer found evidence consistent with the manufacturing of butane hash oil. The affidavit stated that the officer conducted the refuse investigation on Thursday, "regular refuse day." A common-sense reading of the affidavit would indicate that this referred to the most recent Thursday, the date the affidavit was completed. Thus, even if the anonymous tip was so stale as to be unreliable, the marijuana-related items obtained from the refuse search, the defendant's criminal history, and the database searches linking the defendant to the residence provided a substantial basis upon which the magistrate could determine that probable cause existed.

State v. Howard, 259 N.C. App. 848 (2018). The court held that a search warrant was supported by probable cause. Special Agent Wiles obtained a search warrant to search the residence and vehicles at 13606 Coram Place in Charlotte, North Carolina. The agent had twenty-six years of law enforcement experience and had investigated thousands of counterfeit merchandise cases. The warrant application stated that in May 2013, another officer informed the applicant that the defendant was found in possession of possible counterfeit items and was charged with violating the peddlers' license ordinance. The items seized were later confirmed to be counterfeit. In October 2013, as part of a compliance check/counterfeit merchandise interdiction operation at a shipping hub in Charlotte, Wiles intercepted two packages from a known counterfeit merchandise distributor in China that were addressed to the defendant at the residence in question. The boxes contained counterfeit items. Wiles attempted a controlled delivery of the packages at the residence but no one was home. Two other packages previously delivered by the shipper were on the porch. Wiles contacted the defendant, who agreed to meet with him and bring the two packages. The defendant consented to a search of the packages, and they were found to contain counterfeit merchandise. The defendant said that she did not realize the merchandise was counterfeit and voluntarily surrendered all of the merchandise. She was issued a warning. In November 2013, while Wiles was working as part of a compliance check at a football game, the defendant was found selling counterfeit items. The defendant was charged with felony criminal use of counterfeit trademark and pled guilty to the lesser misdemeanor charge. During another compliance check outside of the Charlotte Convention Center in May 2015, Wiles found a booth with a large display of counterfeit items. The booth was unmanned, but business cards listed the owner as "Tammy." Wiles verified that the address listed in the search warrant was the residence of the defendant, Tammy Renee Howard. During a search of the premises pursuant to the warrant, hundreds of counterfeit items with an approximate retail value of $2 million were seized. On appeal, the defendant asserted that the affidavit underlying the warrant application contained insufficient evidence to support a reasonable belief that evidence of counterfeit items would be found at the named premises. The affidavit included evidence of the delivery of counterfeit merchandise to the premises, evidence that the defendant continued to conduct her illegal business after warnings and arrests, and evidence that Agent Wiles confirmed that the defendant resided at the premises. The defendant also argued that the evidence in the affidavit was stale, noting that the only evidence linking the premises with criminal activity allegedly took place in October 2013, some twenty months prior to the issuance of the warrant. However, the evidence showed that the defendant was conducting a business involving counterfeit goods over a number of years at numerous locations and involving the need to acquire counterfeit merchandise from China. For all these reasons, the court ruled that the defendant's motion to suppress evidence obtained in connection with the search was properly denied.

Information from a Confidential Informant (page 486)
Informant's Credibility or the Reliability of the Informant's Information (page 486)
NORTH CAROLINA SUPREME COURT (page 486)

State v. Jackson, 370 N.C. 337 (2017). The supreme court, per curiam and without an opinion, affirmed the ruling of the court of appeals, 249 N.C. App. 642 (2016), that a search warrant was supported by probable cause. At issue was the reliability of information provided by a confidential informant. Applying the totality of the circumstances test, and although the informant did not have a "track record" of providing reliable information, the court found that the informant was sufficiently reliable. The court noted that the information provided by the informant was against her penal interest because, in the course of providing information about her drug supplier, she acknowledged purchasing and possessing marijuana. The court further observed that the informant had a face-to-face communication with the officer to whom she provided information, during which he could assess her demeanor; the face-to-face conversation significantly increased the likelihood that the informant would be held accountable for a tip that later proved to be false; the informant had first-hand knowledge of the information she conveyed; the police independently corroborated certain information she provided regarding the name and address of the supplier; and the information was not stale, as the informant was describing transactions from just two days before.

NORTH CAROLINA COURT OF APPEALS (page 486)

State v. Caddell, ___ N.C. App. ___, ___, ___, 833 S.E.2d 400, 407, 408 (2019). A confidential informant who had provided reliable information in the past told officers that the defendant was selling drugs from his home. The officers had the informant conduct a controlled buy, then obtained a search warrant for the residence. They executed the warrant, found drugs, and charged the defendant with drug trafficking and other offenses. The defendant moved to suppress evidence obtained as a result of the search, a judge denied the motion, and the defendant entered an *Alford* plea and appealed. On appeal, he argued that the search warrant should have been analyzed under the anonymous tip standard and was not supported by probable cause. Under that standard "[a]n anonymous tip, standing alone, is rarely sufficient, but the tip combined with corroboration by the police could show indicia of reliability that would be sufficient to pass constitutional muster." The court ruled that the anonymous tip standard did not apply, as the lead officer "met with [the informant] both before and after the controlled purchase and had worked with [the informant] previously." Furthermore, the controlled buy corroborated the informant's assertions, so the warrant was supported by probable cause.

State v. McPhaul, 256 N.C. App. 303 (2018). The court ruled that a search warrant was supported by probable cause. On appeal, the defendant argued that the warrant lacked probable cause because a statement by a confidential informant provided the only basis to believe that evidence might be found at the premises in question and the supporting affidavit, prepared by Detective Schwab, failed to establish the informant's reliability. The court disagreed. The detective's affidavit detailed a meeting between an officer and the confidential informant in which the informant stated that he witnessed described individuals running from the crime scene and that one of them entered the premises in question. The informant's statement corroborated significant matters previously known to the police department, including the general time and location of the offenses, the victim's physical description of his assailants, and the suspect's possession of items similar in appearance to those stolen from the victim. The affidavit therefore demonstrated the informant's reliability.

State v. Brody, 251 N.C. App. 812, 819 (2017). The court ruled that a search warrant application, prepared by Detective Duft and relying principally upon information obtained from a confidential informant, was sufficient to support a magistrate's finding of probable cause and a subsequent search of the defendant's home. The court rejected the defendant's argument that the affidavit failed to show that the confidential informant was reliable and that drugs were likely to be found in the home. The affidavit stated that investigators had known the confidential informant for two weeks, that the informant had previously provided them with information regarding other people involved in drug trafficking, and that the detective considered the informant reliable. The confidential informant had demonstrated to the detective that he was familiar with drug pricing and with how controlled substances are packaged and sold for distribution. Moreover, the informant had previously arranged and negotiated the purchase of, and did purchase, cocaine from the defendant under the detective's direct supervision, though the warrant application did not extensively detail these transactions. Additionally, the confidential informant told the detective that he had visited the defendant's home approximately thirty times, including within forty-eight hours before the affidavit was prepared, and had seen the defendant possessing and selling cocaine each time. The court noted: "The fact that the affidavit did not describe the precise outcomes of the previous tips from the [informant] did not preclude a determination that the [informant] was reliable." It added: "[A]lthough a general averment that an informant is 'reliable'—taken alone—might raise questions as to the basis for such an assertion," the fact that the detective also specifically stated that investigators had received information from the informant in the past "allows for a reasonable inference that such information demonstrated the [confidential informant's] reliability." Moreover, the detective had further opportunity to gauge his reliability when the informant arranged and negotiated the purchase of, and did purchase, cocaine from the defendant under the detective's supervision.

State v. Kirkman, 251 N.C. App. 274 (2016). The court ruled that a search warrant was properly supported by probable cause. At issue was whether a confidential informant was sufficiently reliable to support a finding of probable cause. The affidavit supporting the warrant noted that the confidential informant was familiar with the appearance of illegal narcotics and that all previous information the informant provided had proven to be truthful and accurate. This information was sufficient to establish the confidential informant's reliability.

Probable Cause for Premises to Be Searched (page 487)

NORTH CAROLINA SUPREME COURT (page 487)

State v. Bailey, 374 N.C. 332 (2020). A detective observed what he believed to be a drug transaction involving a Jeep and another car occur in a parking lot. He knew the occupants of the Jeep and their address. The detective also knew that they previously had been involved in illegal drug sales. Both vehicles were followed by officers. The car was stopped for traffic violations, and the woman inside the car ultimately admitted to having purchased heroin in the parking lot from one of the people inside the Jeep. The Jeep was separately followed to the occupants' residence. Officers obtained a warrant to search the house, and the defendant (who lived at the house but was not one of the Jeep's occupants) was charged with trafficking in cocaine.

The court stated that a search warrant for a residence must demonstrate some nexus between the suspected criminal activity and the home. The connection need not be direct, but it cannot be merely conclusory. The court determined that the search warrant's supporting affidavit in this case established a sufficient connection to the home. The detective saw a possible drug transaction and was familiar with the people in the Jeep, including their drug histories and address. Coupled with the close-in-time admission from the buyer that she purchased heroin from one of the men in the Jeep and the fact that another officer followed that vehicle from the site of the suspected buy to the residence, the affidavit supported an inference that drugs or evidence of drug dealing would be found in the home. The court stated that it was true that the affidavit did not contain any evidence that drugs were actually being sold at the apartment. But case law makes clear that such evidence is unnecessary for probable cause to exist. Rather, the affiant is simply required to demonstrate *some* nexus between a residence and criminal activity. In upholding the search warrant, the court stated that it was not breaking new ground and instead applying well-established legal principles to the facts.

State v. Lewis, 372 N.C. 576 (2019). On discretionary review of a consolidated appeal from two decisions of the court of appeals, 259 N.C. App. 366 (2018), 259 N.C. App. 424 (2018) (unpublished), the supreme court affirmed in part and reversed in part.

A sheriff's deputy arrested Robert Lewis, the defendant, who had been recognized as the possible perpetrator of a string of bank robberies committed over two months. After arresting the defendant, the deputy observed in plain sight a BB&T money bag on the floor of a Kia Optima that matched the description of a vehicle reportedly used to flee the scene of one of the robberies. The deputy also spoke with the defendant's stepfather, who confirmed that the defendant lived at the residence. A detective prepared a search warrant application seeking permission to search the residence where the defendant was arrested, the Kia, and another vehicle reportedly used to flee a different robbery. The affidavit accompanying the search warrant application failed to list several pieces of information. It did not (1) disclose that the defendant lived at the residence; (2) contain any other information linking the defendant to that address; (3) describe the circumstances surrounding his arrest at that address, including that a Kia was parked at the residence then; or (4) mention the deputy's interactions with the defendant or his stepfather, who had confirmed that the defendant lived at the residence. Absent information linking the defendant to the residence, the court ruled that the magistrate lacked probable cause to issue a warrant to search it, and so the court affirmed the court of appeals' ruling that the defendant's motion to suppress evidence obtained from the search should have been granted. A magistrate nonetheless issued the warrant, which led to the seizure of more evidence linking the defendant to the robberies.

The defendant filed multiple motions to suppress, arguing that there was an insufficient connection between the items sought and the property to be searched, and that the search of the Kia was not permissible under the plain view doctrine. The trial court denied the motion. The court of appeals ruled that the detective's search warrant application was sufficient to establish probable cause to search the cars but insufficient to establish probable cause to search the dwelling because the supporting affidavit failed to state that the defendant resided there.

The supreme court noted that the warrant to search the residence—though much of the information in the supporting affidavit linked the defendant to the robberies—failed to set forth the circumstances of the defendant's arrest at this particular address, including how the detective who prepared the warrant initially obtained the address from officers in Johnston County and how the defendant's stepfather had confirmed where the defendant resided. Absent information linking the defendant to the residence, the court ruled that the magistrate lacked probable cause to issue a warrant to search it, and so the court affirmed the court of appeals' ruling that the defendant's motion to suppress should have been granted. Concerning the search of the Kia, the court concluded that the limited information actually set out in the affidavit failed to establish probable cause for the search. As a result, the court reversed the portion of the court of appeals' decision concluding that there was probable cause and remanded the case for consideration of the trial judge's alternative finding that the vehicle search was valid under the plain view doctrine.

State v. Frederick, 371 N.C. 547 (2018). The supreme court affirmed per curiam and without an opinion the ruling of the court of appeals, 259 N.C. App. 165 (2018), that probable cause supported a search warrant. A detective sought a search warrant for the defendant's home. The affidavit in support of the warrant application stated that a "confidential source" had recently given the officer "information . . . regarding a [drug] dealer." The detective considered the source reliable, as he had previously provided accurate information. The detective and the source attempted to corroborate the information by conducting two controlled buys in the week before the warrant application was submitted. In both cases, the informant met with a "middle man," who was apparently unknown to the detective, and took him to the suspect's home. Officers watched the middle man enter the home and exit a few minutes later. The informant dropped the middle man off at his residence and then met with the detective. Each time, the informant had no drugs at the outset and had drugs at the end of the event. A magistrate issued a search warrant based on these transactions, and the court of appeals ruled that probable cause supported the issuance of the search warrant.

State v. Allman, 369 N.C. 292 (2016). Reversing the court of appeals, the court held that a magistrate had a substantial basis to find that probable cause existed to issue a search warrant. The affidavit supporting the warrant stated that an officer stopped a car driven by Jeremy Black. Black's half-brother Sean Whitehead was a passenger. After a K-9 alerted on the car, a search found 8.1 ounces of marijuana and $1,600 in cash. Both individuals had previously been charged on several occasions with drug crimes. Whitehead maintained that the two lived at Twin Oaks Drive in Castle Hayne. The officer went to that address and found that although neither individual lived there, their mother did. The mother informed the officer that the men lived at 4844 Acres Drive in Wilmington and had not lived at Twin Oaks Drive for years. Another officer went to the Acres Drive premises and determined that its description matched that given by the mother and that a truck outside the house was registered to Black. The officer had experience with drug investigations and, based on his training and experience, knew that drug dealers typically keep evidence of drug dealing at their homes. Supported by the affidavit, the officer applied for and received a search warrant to search the Acres Drive home. Drugs and paraphernalia were found. On review, the court found that the warrant was properly issued. Based on the quantity of marijuana and the amount of cash found in the car, the fact that the marijuana appeared to be packaged for sale, and Whitehead's and Black's criminal histories, the magistrate reasonably inferred that the brothers were drug dealers. Based on the mother's statement that the two lived at the Acres Drive premises, the fact that her description of that home matched its actual appearance, and the fact that one of the trucks there was registered to Black, the magistrate reasonably inferred that the two lived there. And based on the insight from the officer's training and experience that evidence of drug dealing was likely to be found at the brothers' home and the fact that Whitehead lied about where the two lived, the magistrate reasonably inferred that there could be evidence of drug dealing at the Acres Drive premises. Although nothing in the affidavit directly connected the defendant's home with evidence of drug dealing, federal circuit courts have held that a suspect drug dealer's lie about his address, in combination with other evidence of drug dealing, can give rise to probable cause to search the suspect's home. Thus, under the totality of the circumstances, there was probable cause to support the search warrant.

NORTH CAROLINA COURT OF APPEALS (page 488)

State v. Howard, 259 N.C. App. 848 (2018). The court held that a search warrant was supported by probable cause. Special Agent Wiles obtained a search warrant to search the residence and vehicles at 13606 Coram Place in Charlotte, North Carolina. The agent had twenty-six years of law enforcement experience and had investigated thousands of counterfeit merchandise cases. The warrant application stated that in May 2013, another officer informed the applicant that the defendant was found in possession of possible counterfeit items and was charged with violating the peddlers' license ordinance. The items seized were later confirmed to be counterfeit. In October 2013, as part of a compliance check/counterfeit merchandise interdiction operation at a shipping hub in Charlotte, Wiles intercepted two packages from a known counterfeit merchandise distributor in China that were addressed to the defendant at the residence in question. The boxes contained counterfeit items. Wiles attempted a controlled delivery of the packages at the residence but no one was home. Two other packages previously delivered by the shipper were on the porch. Wiles contacted the defendant, who agreed to meet with him and bring the two packages. The defendant consented to a search of the packages, and they were found to contain counterfeit merchandise. The defendant said she did not realize the merchandise was counterfeit and voluntarily surrendered all of the merchandise. She was issued a warning. In November 2013, while Wiles was working as part of a compliance check at a football game, the defendant was found selling counterfeit items. The defendant was charged with felony criminal use of counterfeit trademark and pled guilty to the lesser misdemeanor charge. During another compliance check outside of the Charlotte Convention Center in May 2015, Wiles found a booth with a large display of counterfeit items. The booth was unmanned but business cards listed the owner as "Tammy." Wiles verified that the address listed in the search warrant was the residence of the defendant, Tammy Renee Howard. During a search of the premises pursuant to the warrant, hundreds of counterfeit items with an approximate retail value of $2 million were seized. On appeal, the defendant asserted that the affidavit underlying the warrant application contained insufficient evidence to support a reasonable belief that evidence of counterfeit items would be found at the named premises. The affidavit included evidence of the delivery of counterfeit merchandise to the premises, evidence that the defendant continued to conduct her illegal business after warnings and arrests, and evidence that Agent Wiles confirmed that the defendant resided at the premises. The defendant also argued that the evidence in the affidavit was stale, noting that the only evidence linking the premises with criminal activity allegedly took place in October 2013, some twenty months prior to the issuance of the warrant. However, the evidence showed that the defendant was conducting a business involving counterfeit goods over a number of years at numerous locations and involving the need to acquire counterfeit merchandise from China. For all these reasons, the defendant's motion to suppress evidence obtained in connection with the search was properly denied.

State v. Worley, 254 N.C. App. 572, 573 (2017). The court ruled that the trial court properly denied the defendant's motion to suppress evidence seized pursuant to search warrants for his rental cabin and truck. The defendant argued that the search warrant application established no nexus between the cabin and the criminal activity—the theft of goods during a breaking and entering of a horse trailer. The court found, however, "that under the totality of the circumstances, the accumulation of reasonable inferences drawn from information contained within the affidavit sufficiently linked the criminal activity to defendant's cabin." Among other things, the affidavit established that when one of the owners of the horse trailer hired the defendant to work at her farm, several tools and pieces of equipment went missing and were never recovered; immediately before the defendant moved out of state, someone broke into the car of the property owners' daughter and stole property; the defendant rented a cabin close to the owners' property around the same time as the reported breaking and entering and larceny; and the defendant had prior convictions for first-degree burglary and felony larceny. Based on this and other evidence discussed in detail in the court's opinion, the affidavit established a sufficient nexus between the criminal activity and the defendant's cabin.

State v. Parson, 250 N.C. App. 142 (2016). The court ruled that the trial court erred by denying the defendant's motion to suppress evidence seized pursuant to a search warrant. The court found that the application for the search warrant insufficiently connected the address in question to the objects sought. It noted that none of the allegations in the affidavit specifically referred to the address in question and none established the required nexus between the objects sought (evidence of manufacturing methamphetamine) and the place to be searched. The court further stated that the defendant's refusal of an officer's request to search the property cannot establish probable cause to search.

Search Warrants for Computers (page 495)

NORTH CAROLINA SUPREME COURT (page 495)

State v. Terrell, 372 N.C. 657, 659 (2019). The court ruled that an officer's warrantless search of a defendant's thumb drive following a prior search by a private individual violated the defendant's Fourth Amendment rights. While examining a thumb drive belonging to the defendant, the defendant's girlfriend saw an image of her 9-year-old granddaughter sleeping, exposed from the waist up. Believing the image was inappropriate, the girlfriend contacted the sheriff's office and gave them the thumb drive. Later, a detective conducted a warrantless search of the thumb drive to locate the image in question, during which he discovered other images of what he believed to be child pornography before he found the photograph of the granddaughter. At that point the detective applied for and obtained a warrant to search the contents of the thumb drive for "contraband images of child pornography and evidence of additional victims and crimes." The initial warrant application relied only on information from the defendant's girlfriend, but after the State Bureau of Investigation (SBI) requested additional information, the detective included information about the images he found in his initial search of the USB drive. The SBI's forensic examination turned up twelve images, ten of which had been deleted and archived in a way that would not have been viewable without special forensic capabilities.

The court concluded that the girlfriend opening the thumb drive and viewing some of its contents did not frustrate the defendant's privacy interest in the entire contents of the device. To the contrary, digital devices can retain massive amounts of information, organized into files that are essentially containers within containers. Because the trial court did not make findings establishing the precise scope of the girlfriend's search, it likewise could not find that the detective had the level of "virtual certainty" contemplated by *United States v. Jacobsen*, 466 U.S. 109 (1984), that the device contained nothing else of significance or that a subsequent search would not tell him anything more than he already had been told. The search therefore was not permissible under the private-search doctrine. The court affirmed the decision of the court of appeals, 257 N.C. App. 884 (2018), and remanded the case for consideration of whether the warrant would have been supported by probable cause without the evidence obtained through the unlawful search.

Search Warrants for Obscene Materials (page 497)

NORTH CAROLINA COURT OF APPEALS (page 498)

State v. Gerard, 249 N.C. App. 500 (2016). In this sexual exploitation of a minor case, the information contained in an officer's affidavit was sufficient to provide probable cause for issuance of a search warrant for child pornography. An officer and certified computer forensic examiner identified images possessed by the defendant as child pornography through the use of an SHA1 algorithm or hash value, which the court noted is an "algorithm" that is "like a fingerprint" that may be used to identify digital files. Although less detailed than the officer's testimony at the hearing, the affidavit described technical detail regarding law enforcement methods and software used to identify and track transmissions of child pornography over the Internet. The court rejected the defendant's argument that the affidavit's identification of alleged pornographic images as known child pornography based upon computer information was insufficient and that the pictures themselves must be provided with the affidavit.

Executing a Search Warrant (page 498)

Notice and Entry (page 498)

NORTH CAROLINA COURT OF APPEALS (page 501)

State v. Winchester, 260 N.C. App. 418 (2018). The court rejected the defendant's argument that the search of his residence the premises was unreasonable. The defendant argued that because the officers deliberately waited until he vacated the premises before breaking open the door without knocking and announcing their presence, they violated the statutory knock-and-announce requirement. Here, before executing the search warrant a detective loudly announced three times that officers would be entering the residence to execute the search warrant. After waiting a reasonable time and hearing no response, officers made a forced entry into the residence. These facts established that a statutory violation did not occur.

People Present during the Execution of a Search Warrant (page 502)
Detaining People Present (page 502)
NORTH CAROLINA SUPREME COURT (page 503)

State v. Wilson, 371 N.C. 920, 921, 925 (2018) (internal quotation marks, citation omitted). The court ruled that *Michigan v. Summers,* 452 U.S. 692 (1981), justified a seizure of the defendant when he posed a real threat to the safe and efficient completion of a search warrant execution and that the later search of the defendant was supported by individualized suspicion. A SWAT team was sweeping a house so that the police could execute a search warrant. Several officers were positioned around the house to create a perimeter securing the scene. The defendant penetrated the SWAT perimeter, stating that he was going to get his moped. In so doing, he passed Officer Christian, who was stationed at the perimeter near the street. The defendant then kept going, moving up the driveway and towards the house to be searched. Officer Ayers, who was stationed near the house, confronted the defendant. After a brief interaction, Officer Ayers searched the defendant based on his suspicion that the defendant was armed. Officer Ayers found a firearm in the defendant's pocket. The defendant, who had previously been convicted of a felony, was arrested and charged with being a felon in possession of a firearm. He unsuccessfully moved to suppress evidence of the firearm at trial and was convicted.

The court of appeals ruled that the search was invalid because the trial court's order did not show that the search was supported by reasonable suspicion. The supreme court reversed. It ruled that "the rule in *Michigan v. Summers* justified the seizure here because the defendant, who passed one officer, stated he was going to get his moped, and continued toward the premises being searched, posed a real threat to the safe and efficient completion of the search." The court interpreted the *Summers* rule to mean that a warrant to search for contraband founded on probable cause implicitly carries with it the limited authority to detain occupants who are within the immediate vicinity of the premises to be searched and who are present during the execution of a search warrant. Applying this rule, the court determined that "a person is an occupant for the purposes of the *Summers* rule if he poses a real threat to the safe and efficient execution of a search warrant." (citation omitted). Here, the defendant posed such a threat. The court reasoned: "He approached the house being swept, announced his intent to retrieve his moped from the premises, and appeared to be armed. It was obvious that defendant posed a threat to the safe completion of the search."

Because the *Summers* rule only justifies detentions incident to the execution of search warrants, the court went on to considering whether the later search of the defendant's person was justified. On this issue the court held that search of the defendant was supported by individualized suspicion and thus did not violate the Fourth Amendment.

Service of a Search Warrant and Completion of an Inventory (page 506)
NORTH CAROLINA COURT OF APPEALS (page 506)

State v. Downey, 249 N.C. App. 415, 426 (2016). The court rejected the defendant's argument that the trial court erred by denying his motion to suppress evidence collected from his residence during the execution of a search warrant on the grounds that the inventory list prepared by one of the officers who executed the warrant was unlawfully vague and inaccurate in describing the items seized. The defendant argued that the evidence gathered from his residence was obtained in substantial violation of G.S. 15A-254, which requires an officer executing a search warrant to write and sign a receipt itemizing the items taken. However, in order for suppression to be warranted for a substantial violation of G.S. Chapter 15A, G.S. 15A-974 requires (1) that the evidence be obtained as a result of an officer's unlawful conduct and (2) that it would not have been obtained but for the unlawful conduct. Here, citing prior case law, the court held, in part, that because the evidence was seized before the inventory required by the statute had to be prepared, the defendant failed to show that the evidence would not have been obtained but for the alleged violations of G.S. 15A-254. The court held that G.S. 15A-254 "applies only after evidence has been obtained and does not implicate the right to be free from unreasonable search and seizure. In turn, because evidence cannot be obtained 'as a result of' a violation of [G.S.] 15A-254, [G.S.] 15A-974(a)(2) is inapplicable to either alleged or actual [G.S.] 15A-254 violations."

Scope of the Search and Seizure with a Search Warrant (page 508)
Searching Vehicles Not Named in the Warrant (page 511)
NORTH CAROLINA SUPREME COURT (page 511)

State v. Lowe, 369 N.C. 360, 367–68 (2016). The state supreme court held that a search of a vehicle located within the curtilage of a residence was within the scope of a search warrant for the home even though the vehicle in question was a rental car in the possession of the defendant, an overnight guest at the house. The court stated that if a search warrant validly describes the premises to be searched, a car on the premises may be searched even though the warrant contains no description of the car. In departing from this general rule, the court of appeals had held that the search of the car was invalid because the officers who executed the search warrant knew that the vehicle in question did not belong to the suspect in the drug investigation. Noting that the record was unclear as to what the officers knew about ownership and control of the vehicle, the supreme court concluded: "[R]egardless of whether the officers knew the car was a rental, we hold that the search was within the scope of the warrant."

III. Nontestimonial Identification Procedures and Orders (page 526)

Authority to Conduct Nontestimonial Identification Procedures (page 531)
Using Force to Take Blood (page 532)
NORTH CAROLINA COURT OF APPEALS (page 532)

State v. Hoque, ___ N.C. App. ___, 837 S.E.2d 464 (2020). When the defendant refused to take an Intoxilyzer test, an officer obtained a search warrant to take a blood sample from him. When the defendant resisted a hospital nurse's attempts to take a blood sample, officers pinned the defendant to a bed. The court ruled that the force used was reasonable under Fourth Amendment.

IV. Suppression Motions and Hearings; Exclusionary Rules (page 534)

General Exclusionary Rules (page 550)
Derivative Evidence: Fruit of the Poisonous Tree (page 551)
NORTH CAROLINA COURT OF APPEALS (page 552)

State v. Thomas, ___ N.C. App. ___, ___, ___, ___, 834 S.E.2d 654, 659, 661, 662 (2019) (citations omitted). The defendant was convicted of four counts of first-degree murder and other charges. He argued that the trial court erred in denying his motion to suppress all evidence obtained as a result of a device placed on his cell phone, but the court of appeals affirmed.

The offenses alleged occurred in 2005, although the defendant was not tried until 2017. As a part of the investigation into the homicides and other crimes with which the defendant was charged, law enforcement officers obtained an order authorizing the use of a pen register to obtain sixty days of cell-site location information (CSLI) on a phone connected to the defendant in 2005. The officers acted under G.S. 15A-262, which requires a showing only of "relevance" to an investigation, and did not obtain a search warrant. The defendant alleged this violated *Carpenter v. United States*, 585 U.S. ___, 138 S. Ct. 2206 (2018). Rejecting this argument, the court first noted *Carpenter's* scope: "*Carpenter* only established the government must obtain a warrant before it can access a phone company's *historical* CSLI; it did not extend its holding to the issue of government acquisition of real-time or prospective CSLI." Here, the State sought both types of data, and it was unclear which category of information was used to actually locate the defendant. *Carpenter* would only control as to the historical data (but the case did, indeed, apply to that category of data, despite having been decided thirteen years after the events in question, because *Carpenter* was decided while this matter was on direct appeal).

Here, it was unnecessary to decide the extent of protections for real-time or prospective CSLI, given that the evidence was sufficiently attenuated from any illegality (an alternative ground found by the trial court to justify the search). "Evidence is admissible when the connection between unconstitutional police conduct and the evidence is remote or has been interrupted by some intervening circumstance, so that 'the interest protected by the constitutional guarantee that has been violated would not be served by suppression of the evidence obtained,'" the court found. It continued:

> The [United States] Supreme Court has identified three factors to aid in determining whether there was a sufficient intervening event to break the casual link between the government's unlawful act and the discovery of evidence: (1) the "temporal proximity" of the unconstitutional conduct and the discovery of evidence, (2) the "presence of intervening circumstances," and (3) "particularly, the purpose and flagrancy of the official misconduct."

Here, three days had passed between the court order authorizing the CSLI and law enforcement locating the defendant. That amount of time was not substantial and weighed in favor of suppression. However, the intervening circumstances here weighed heavily in favor of attenuation—the defendant was found with guns and ammo, threatened to shoot at officers when they attempted to apprehend him, and actually fired a gun at officers during the course of his arrest. The court stated that "this constituted an intervening circumstance sufficient to attenuate the connection between any unconstitutional police conduct and the discovery of evidence." Finally, the court found that the purpose of the exclusionary rule would not be served by suppression here because the misconduct was "neither purposeful nor flagrant." Officers acted according to the law and common understanding of pen registers in 2005, and no reasons existed then to believe that those procedures were unconstitutional. The court ruled that the trial court therefore did not err in denying the defendant's motion to suppress.

State v. Burwell, 256 N.C. App. 722, 728, 729, 730 (2017) (citations omitted). The court ruled that the trial court did not err by denying the defendant's motion to suppress evidence of his attack on a law enforcement officer, which the defendant alleged was proper resistance to an unlawful arrest. The court concluded that "[e]ven if a police officer's conduct violates a defendant's Fourth Amendment rights, evidence of an attack on an officer is not fruit of a poisonous tree subject to suppression." It elaborated:

> "The doctrine of the fruit of the poisonous tree is a specific application of the exclusionary rule[,]" providing for the suppression of "all evidence obtained as a result of illegal police conduct." However, this doctrine does not permit evidence of attacks on police officers to be excluded, even "where those attacks occur while the officers are engaging in conduct that violates a defendant's Fourth Amendment rights." Thus, where a defendant argues an initial stop or subsequent arrest violated "his Fourth Amendment rights, the evidence of his crimes against the officers would not be considered excludable 'fruits' pursuant to the doctrine."

Here, the defendant sought suppression of evidence of an attack on a police officer. The court concluded: "Defendant seeks the suppression of evidence of an attack on a police officer. Since evidence of an attack on a police officer cannot be suppressed as a fruit of the poisonous tree, the evidence Defendant sought to suppress cannot be suppressed as a matter of law."

State v. Hester, 254 N.C. App. 506 (2017). The court held that even if the initial stop of the defendant by Deputy Cranford was not supported by reasonable suspicion, the trial court properly denied the defendant's motion to suppress when the evidence sought to be suppressed—a stolen handgun—was obtained after the defendant committed a separate crime: pointing a loaded gun at the deputy and pulling the trigger. The evidence at issue was admissible under the attenuation doctrine, which holds that evidence is admissible when the connection between the unconstitutional police conduct and the evidence is remote or has been interrupted by some intervening circumstance, so that the interest protected by the constitutional guarantee that has been violated would not be served by suppression. Here, the defendant's commission of a crime broke any causal chain between the presumably unlawful stop and the discovery of the stolen handgun.

The Inevitable Discovery Exception (page 556)
NORTH CAROLINA COURT OF APPEALS (page 557)

State v. Jackson, 262 N.C. App. 329, 338 (2018) (citation omitted). This case involved a traffic stop, a search of the defendant's pockets, and later drug charges and a charge of driving without an operator's license. The court ruled that evidence of the discovery of cocaine on the defendant's person, even if the search violated the Fourth Amendment, would have been admissible under the inevitable discovery exception. Under this exception, "evidence which is illegally obtained can still be admitted into evidence as an exception to the exclusionary rule when the information ultimately or inevitably would have been discovered by lawful means." The officer who stopped the defendant testified that he would not have allowed the defendant to drive away from the traffic stop because he was not licensed to operate a motor vehicle. Instead, he would have searched the defendant before giving him a ride or transporting him to jail because of his practice of searching everyone being transported in his patrol car. Also, the defendant repeatedly asked the officer if he would give him a ride back to a hotel. Thus, the State established that the cocaine would have been inevitably discovered because the officer would have searched the defendant for weapons or contraband before transporting him to another location or to jail.

Chapter 5

Interrogation and Confessions, Lineups and Other Identification Procedures, and Undercover Officers and Informants

Part I. Interrogation and Confessions (page 565)

Unconstitutional Seizure and the Resulting Statement (page 566)

One specific scenario that arises with some frequency involves an officer's decision to question a motorist, stopped for a traffic violation, about the motorist's suspected involvement in criminal activity. The extent to which an officer may do so is addressed in a recent School of Government publication, Shea Riggsbee Denning, Christopher Tyner, and Jeffrey B. Welty, *Pulled Over: The Law of Traffic Stops and Offenses in North Carolina* 60–61 (2017).

Recording Custodial Interrogations at a Place of Detention (page 567)

The main text notes on page 567, in footnote 13, that Section 211 of G.S. Chapter 15A requires the recording of "all custodial interrogations of juveniles in criminal investigations conducted at any place of detention," and explains the uncertainty regarding whether "juvenile" for this purpose means a person under age 16 (the age of criminal juvenile jurisdiction under then-existing law) or a person under age 18 (the general legal meaning of the term). The Juvenile Justice Reinvestment Act, effective for offenses committed on or after December 1, 2019, commonly known as the "raise the age" law, raised the age of juvenile jurisdiction to 18 for most cases and eliminates this conflict.[1] Now, the better reading of the term "juvenile" in G.S. 15A-211 clearly is a person under age 18.

---

1. *See generally* S.L. 2017-57, § 16D.4. Not included in "most cases," for example, are all Chapter 20 motor vehicle offenses committed by a person at age 16 or 17 that remain under the original jurisdiction of the adult court. Jacquelyn Greene, *Raise the Age Tips and Resources for Law Enforcement*, UNC Sch. of Gov't: N.C. Crim. L. Blog (Nov. 26, 2019), https://nccriminallaw.sog.unc.edu/raise-the-age-tips-and-resources-for-law-enforcement/. See the definition of *delinquent juvenile* in G.S. 7B-1501(7). See also G.S. 7B-1604(b), which places limitations on juvenile court jurisdiction. It provides that any juvenile under 18 years old must be prosecuted as an adult for any criminal offense the juvenile commits after a district or superior court conviction if (1) the juvenile has previously been transferred to and convicted in superior court; or (2) the juvenile has previously been convicted in either district or superior court for a felony or misdemeanor; however, any violation of motor vehicle laws punishable as a misdemeanor or infraction is not considered a conviction unless it was for impaired driving or commercial impaired driving.

Voluntariness of the Defendant's Statement (page 569)

In *State v. Johnson*,[2] the North Carolina Supreme Court ruled that the defendant's statements to officers were voluntary. The defendant voluntarily met with detectives at the police station in connection with a robbery and murder. He was questioned in an interview room for just under five hours before being placed under arrest and warned of his *Miranda* rights. After being advised of his rights, the defendant signed a written waiver of those rights and made inculpatory statements. He was charged with first-degree felony murder. At trial, he sought to suppress his statements to officers, arguing that he was subjected to custodial interrogation before being informed of his *Miranda* rights and that his inculpatory statements were involuntarily made under the Due Process Clause in response to improper statements by detectives inducing a hope that his confession would benefit him. The trial court denied his motion and he was convicted. On appeal, the court of appeals concluded that the defendant's inculpatory statements to law enforcement were given under the influence of fear or hope caused by the interrogating officers' statements and actions and were therefore involuntarily made and inadmissible. However, the court of appeals ruled that the error was harmless beyond a reasonable doubt due to the overwhelming evidence of the defendant's guilt.

The supreme court ruled that (1) the court of appeals erred in condensing the *Miranda* and voluntariness inquiries into one; (2) the defendant did not preserve the argument that officers employed the "question first, warn later" technique to obtain his confession in violation of *Miranda* and *Missouri v. Seibert*, 542 U.S. 600 (2004); and (3) the trial court's conclusion that the *Miranda* requirements were met was adequately supported by its findings of fact, as was its conclusion that the defendant's statements to officers were voluntarily made. The supreme court thus modified and affirmed the court of appeals ruling.

In *State v. Lynch*,[3] the 18-year-old defendant was convicted of first-degree murder and other offenses and sentenced to life imprisonment without parole. The case arose from a robbery of a bar by two masked people, during which the bar owner was shot and killed and after which the assailants fled with the cash register. The defendant was later arrested and waived his *Miranda* rights. The defendant adamantly denied his involvement throughout much of the three-hour recorded interrogation, but near the end he confessed to his involvement. The confession was introduced at his trial. The defendant argued on appeal that his confession was involuntarily given because it was induced by the hope of a sentence of life imprisonment instilled by the interrogating officers' statements and actions.

The court of appeals reviewed the transcript of the confession and concluded that, based on the totality of the circumstances, the defendant's confession was involuntary. The court found that (1) the defendant was predisposed to deny involvement and believed that he would receive a life sentence whether or not he confessed and (2) without being prompted by the defendant, the officers introduced the idea that they had ample evidence against the defendant, they knew he was lying, the judge could be influenced to show leniency if he confessed, and they would be willing to testify on his behalf. The court also found that the constitutional error in admitting the confession was not harmless beyond a reasonable doubt.

The *Miranda* Rule and Additional Statutory Rights (page 570)

Overview (page 570)

A Young Arrestee's Additional Statutory Warnings and Rights (page 572)

There has been considerable litigation concerning the statutory rights of young arrestees since the publication of the main text. In *State v. Benitez*,[4] the court ruled that a guardianship is a relationship that must be established through a "legal process." In other words, an adult is not a "guardian" of a young person simply

---

2. 371 N.C. 870 (2018), *modifying and affirming the court of appeals ruling at* 251 N.C. App. 639 (2017).

3. ___ N.C. App. ___, 843 S.E.2d 346 (2020).

4. 258 N.C. App. 491 (2018).

because the two are related (in *Benitez*, the adult was the child's uncle) and live together, and simply because the adult takes care of the young person's needs such as food, shelter, and school enrollment.

In *State v. Saldierna*,[5] the court ruled that a juvenile who wants to assert his or her right to have a parent, guardian, or custodian present when he or she is undergoing custodial interrogation by law enforcement must do so unambiguously, just as an adult arrestee who wants to assert his or her *Miranda* rights must do so unambiguously. The case involved a 16-year-old's question, "Um, can I call my mom?" The state supreme court ruled that the remark was "at best an ambiguous invocation of his right to have his mother present"[6] that did not require officers to cease questioning or even seek clarification regarding the juvenile's wishes. In later litigation involving defendant Saldierna's case, the court ruled[7] that the evidence supported the trial judge's finding that the juvenile knowingly and voluntarily waived his juvenile rights.

When the *Miranda* Rule Applies: Custody and Interrogation (page 573)
The Meaning of "Custody" (page 573)
The seizure of a person under the Fourth Amendment (page 574)
Additional recent cases illustrating that not every seizure amounts to custody include *State v. Burris*[8] and *State v. Barnes*.[9]

NEW SECTION: Person subject to involuntary commitment (page 576)
A person confined under a civil commitment order may be considered in custody for *Miranda* purposes, at least under certain circumstances. In *State v. Hammonds*, the court ruled that the defendant was in custody while "confined under a civil commitment order."[10] He was a suspect in an armed robbery, but shortly after the robbery, as a result of a drug overdose, he was confined at a hospital based upon a magistrate's determination that he was "mentally ill and dangerous to self or others."[11] Officers questioned him about the robbery without informing him of his *Miranda* rights, and he made incriminating statements. His motion to suppress those statements was denied by the trial court, but the state supreme court ultimately reversed. It noted that the defendant's freedom of movement was severely restricted by the civil commitment order, that the officers failed to inform him that he was free to terminate the questioning, and that the officers indicated that they would leave only after he spoke to them about the robbery. The court ruled that, considering all the circumstances, "these statements, made to a suspect whose freedom is already severely restricted because of an involuntary commitment, would lead a reasonable person in this position to believe 'he was not at liberty to terminate the interrogation' without first answering his interrogators' questions about his suspected criminal activity."[12]

Waiver of *Miranda* Rights (page 578)
A relatively recent North Carolina case finding an implied waiver is *State v. Knight*,[13] where the defendant was read his *Miranda* rights, then talked at length with the officers without expressly acknowledging or waiving his rights. The state supreme court, applying *Berghuis v. Thompkins*,[14] found that there was no *Miranda* violation,

---

5. 369 N.C. 401 (2016).

6. *Id.* at 409.

7. State v. Saldierna, 371 N.C. 407 (2018). The court reversed a contrary ruling of the court of appeals, 254 N.C. App. 446 (2017).

8. 253 N.C. App. 525 (2017) (ruling that the defendant was not in custody for *Miranda* purposes just because an officer had detained him and was in possession of his driver's license).

9. 248 N.C. App. 388 (2016) (ruling that although the defendant was detained in handcuffs at the time he was questioned, he was not, based on the totality of the circumstances, "in custody" for purposes of *Miranda*; the handcuffs were used for "officer safety" while a parole officer searched the defendant's cousin's house).

10. 370 N.C. 158, 159 (2017).

11. *Id.*

12. *Id.* at 166 (citation omitted).

13. 369 N.C. 640 (2017).

14. 560 U.S. 370 (2010).

as the defendant understood his *Miranda* rights and effected an implied waiver by choosing to speak with the officers. The court specifically rejected the idea that an express acknowledgment, statement of understanding, or waiver was required, instead applying a totality of the circumstances analysis.

Part II. Lineups and Other Identification Procedures (page 594)

Introduction (page 594)
Juveniles (page 594)
Regarding what age renders a suspect a juvenile for purposes of conducting nontestimonial identification procedures, see page 63 of this supplement.

Nonsuggestiveness of the Identification Procedure under Due Process Clause (page 595)

Although most of the cases concerning suggestive identification procedures involve field identification procedures conducted by officers, in *State v. Malone*[15] the North Carolina Supreme Court ruled that identifications by two eyewitnesses to a shooting committed by two suspects were tainted by a trial preparation meeting between the two eyewitnesses and a legal assistant from the district attorney's office.

The eyewitnesses viewed photo lineups two days after the shooting. The two women identified one of the suspects, who was not the defendant. However, they were unable to identify the other suspect, the defendant, who was tried and convicted as the other person involved in the shooting. For three and a half years the eyewitnesses had no contact with the State until the legal assistant met them at the courthouse for trial preparation. She showed them the defendant's recorded interview with officers and photos of the defendant. One of the women looked out the window and saw the defendant, in a jail uniform and handcuffs, being led into the courthouse for a hearing. She immediately stated that he was one of the killers. The other woman came to the window and also saw the defendant. Both women later identified the defendant at trial as one of the perpetrators. The state supreme court ruled that the trial-preparation session was an "impermissibly suggestive" identification procedure. Given that the women had not previously identified the defendant as a participant in the crime, the legal assistant's "actions in showing [the women] the video of [the defendant's] interview and recent photographs . . . are exactly the kind of highly suggestive procedures that have been widely condemned as inherently suggestive" and amounted to improper witness coaching.[16] However, the court found that the procedure did not give "rise to a substantial likelihood of irreparable misidentification . . . because the trial court's findings of fact support the legal conclusion that [one of the women's] in-court identification of defendant was of independent origin and sufficiently reliable."[17] Among other factors, the court highlighted the woman's proximity to the perpetrators, her opportunity to observe them, and the fact that when she saw a picture of the defendant online shortly after the crime—wearing his hair in a style different from his lineup photo and apparently more similar to his appearance at the time of the crime—she identified him as a perpetrator. Because one of the women made a valid in-court identification, any error in admitting the other woman's in-court identification of the defendant was harmless beyond a reasonable doubt.

---

15. 373 N.C. 134 (2019). The court affirmed in part and reversed in part the rulings of the court of appeals, 256 N.C. App. 275 (2017).

16. *Id.* at 148.

17. *Id.* at 149.

North Carolina Statutory Procedures for Live Lineups and Photo Lineups (page 598)

On page 598 of the main text, in footnote 169, the citation to S.L. 2007-434 should instead be to S.L. 2007-421.

On page 599 of the main text, in the paragraph beginning with "The term 'showup' is defined as a procedure in which an eyewitness . . .," add a new bullet as follows:

- Despite G.S. 7B-2103 (generally requiring a nontestimonial identification order to conduct a nontestimonial identification procedure), an officer must photograph a juvenile suspect who is 10 years of age or older at the time and place of the show-up if the juvenile is reported to have committed a nondivertible offense under G.S. 7B-1701[18] or common law robbery. G.S. 15A-284.52(c1) also sets out duties concerning the retention or disposal of any photos and who may examine them and under what conditions.[19]

On page 599 of the main text, at the end of the first sentence in the paragraph beginning with "Third, when evidence of compliance or noncompliance has been presented at trial . . .", insert a footnote with note text that reads as follows: "In *State v. Reaves-Smith*, ___ N.C. App ___, 844 S.E.2d 19 (2020), the defendant argued on appeal that he was entitled to a jury instruction on noncompliance with the statutes because the officer did not obtain an eyewitness confidence statement required under G.S. 15A-284.52(c2)(2), but the court rejected that argument on the ground that G.S. 15A-284.52(c2) concerns policies and guidelines established by the North Carolina Criminal Justice Education and Training Standards Commission, not the requirements for show-up identifications. Because the officers complied with the show-up procedures in G.S. 15A-284.52(c1), the defendant was not entitled to a jury instruction on noncompliance with the statutes."

---

18. The nondivertible offenses are murder, first-degree rape and sexual offense, second-degree rape and sexual offense, arson, any felony violation of Article 5 (Controlled Substances Act) of G.S. Chapter 90, first-degree burglary, crime against nature, and any felony that involves the willful infliction of serious bodily injury on another or that is committed with the use of a deadly weapon.

19. S.L. 2019-47, effective June 17, 2019.

Chapter 5 Appendix: Case Summaries

I. Interrogation and Confessions (page 609)

Voluntariness of the Defendant's Statement (page 609)
Generally (page 609)
NORTH CAROLINA SUPREME COURT (page 610)

State v. Johnson, 371 N.C. 870 (2018). The North Carolina Supreme Court ruled that the defendant's statements to officers were voluntary. The defendant voluntarily met with detectives at the police station in connection with a robbery and murder. He was questioned in an interview room for just under five hours before being placed under arrest and warned of his *Miranda* rights. After being advised of his rights, the defendant signed a written waiver of those rights and made inculpatory statements. He was charged with first-degree felony murder. At trial, he sought to suppress his statements to officers, arguing that he was subjected to custodial interrogation before being informed of his *Miranda* rights and that his inculpatory statements were involuntarily made under the Due Process Clause in response to improper statements by detectives inducing a hope that his confession would benefit him. The trial court denied his motion and he was convicted. On appeal, the court of appeals concluded that the defendant's inculpatory statements to law enforcement were given under the influence of fear or hope caused by the interrogating officers' statements and actions and were therefore involuntarily made and inadmissible. However, the court ruled that the error was harmless beyond a reasonable doubt due to the overwhelming evidence of the defendant's guilt. The state supreme court held that (1) the court of appeals erred in condensing the *Miranda* and voluntariness inquiries into one; (2) the defendant did not preserve the argument that officers employed the "question first, warn later" technique to obtain his confession in violation of *Miranda* and *Missouri v. Seibert,* 542 U.S. 600 (2004); and (3) the trial court's conclusion that the *Miranda* requirements were met was adequately supported by its findings of fact, as was its conclusion that the defendant's statements to officers were voluntarily made. The supreme court thus modified and affirmed the ruling of the court of appeals.

Defendant's Statements: *Miranda* Warnings and Waiver (page 616)
Waiver of *Miranda* Rights (page 621)
Generally (page 621)
NORTH CAROLINA SUPREME COURT (page 623)

State v. Knight, 369 N.C. 640 (2017). The defendant was arrested for rape, and officers read him his *Miranda* rights. He did not expressly acknowledge or waive them, but talked at length with the officers, attempting to convince them of his innocence but in fact making statements that eventually became part of the State's case against him. He moved to suppress the statements prior to trial but his motion was denied. After he was convicted, he appealed. The court of appeals found a *Miranda* violation because the defendant did not expressly waive his rights, though a majority of the court saw it as harmless. The state supreme court, applying *Berghuis v. Thompkins,* 560 U.S. 370 (2010), found that there was no *Miranda* violation, as the defendant understood his *Miranda* rights and effected an implied waiver by choosing to speak with the officers. The court noted that the defendant was an adult who spoke English fluently and had his rights read to him, so there was no doubt that he understood them. And it rejected the idea that an express acknowledgment, statement of understanding, or waiver was required, instead applying a totality of the circumstances analysis.

NORTH CAROLINA COURT OF APPEALS (page 624)

State v. Santillan, 259 N.C. App. 394, 401 (2018). Police arrested a 15-year-old suspect in connection with a double murder. He initially waived his right to counsel but later asserted it, leading the officers to stop questioning him. He then had a brief exchange with the chief of police in which, among other things, the chief told him that he had "f***** up." The defendant subsequently waived his right to counsel again and made further statements. His motion to suppress those statements was denied, and they were admitted against him at trial. The court of appeals remanded for further findings regarding whether the conversation with the chief was an unlawful attempt to interrogate an arrestee who had asserted his right to counsel. The court rejected the defendant's argument that "his second waiver [of his right to counsel] was involuntary because of factors including his young age, the officers' interrogation tactics, and his lack of sleep, food, and medication." The court agreed with the trial judge that the defendant's "actions and statements show[ed] awareness and cognitive reasoning during the entire interview" and that the defendant "was not coerced into making any statements, but rather made his statements voluntarily."

The Meaning of "Custody" under *Miranda* (page 630)

Generally (page 630)

NORTH CAROLINA SUPREME COURT (page 633)

State v. Hammonds, 370 N.C. 158, 159, 166 (2017) (citation omitted). The defendant was in custody for *Miranda* purposes while "confined under a civil commitment order." He was a suspect in an armed robbery, but shortly after the robbery, as a result of a drug overdose, he was confined at a hospital based upon a magistrate's determination that he was "mentally ill and dangerous to self or others." Officers questioned him about the robbery without informing him of his *Miranda* rights, and he made incriminating statements. His motion to suppress those statements was denied by the trial court, but the state supreme court ultimately reversed. It noted that the defendant's freedom of movement was severely restricted by the civil commitment order, that the officers failed to inform him that he was free to terminate the questioning, and that the officers indicated that they would leave only after he spoke to them about the robbery. The court ruled that, considering all the circumstances, "these statements, made to a suspect whose freedom is already severely restricted because of an involuntary commitment, would lead a reasonable person in this position to believe he 'was not at liberty to terminate the interrogation' without first answering his interrogators' questions about his suspected criminal activity." For a more complete discussion of *Hammonds*, see Bob Farb, *New North Carolina Appellate Cases on the Meaning of Custody under Miranda v. Arizona*, UNC SCH. OF GOV'T: N.C. CRIM. L. BLOG (June 14, 2016), https://nccriminallaw.sog.unc.edu/new-north-carolina-appellate-cases-meaning-custody-miranda-v-arizona/.

NORTH CAROLINA COURT OF APPEALS (page 637)

State v. Gamez, 264 N.C. App. 467, 489 (2019) (footnote omitted). The defendant, a U.S. Army private, was charged with second-degree murder, aiding and abetting a first-degree kidnapping, and conspiracy to kidnap. Concerning the defendant's oral statement made to Schlegelmilch, a non-commissioned first sergeant in the U.S. Army, the court vacated and remanded because it found that the trial court (1) did not make factual findings on several issues integral to the question of whether a *Miranda* violation had occurred and (2) failed to fully apply the correct legal standard applicable to the issue. The defendant argued that because he was interrogated by a superior officer who had the power to arrest him, a custodial interrogation occurred. The State countered that a custodial arrest does not occur unless the soldier is questioned by a commissioned officer with independent arrest authority. Citing federal law, the court noted that a commanding officer may delegate arrest authority to a non-commissioned officer. When this has occurred, the non-commissioned officer's interrogation of the soldier can trigger the need for *Miranda* warnings. Here, it is undisputed that Schlegelmilch was a non-commissioned officer. Therefore, to resolve the issue of whether the defendant was entitled to *Miranda* warnings, it was necessary to determine whether Schlegelmilch previously had been delegated authority to arrest the defendant by a commanding officer as authorized by federal law. However, the trial court did not make any findings as to whether such a delegation occurred. Additionally, the trial court's order suggests that it failed to understand the potential applicability of *Miranda* if Schlegelmilch had, in fact, been delegated authority to arrest and then proceeded to question the defendant under circumstances amounting to custodial interrogation. Nor did the trial court make findings about the specific degree to which the defendant's liberty had been restricted when he made the statements. The court thus vacated the portion of the trial court's suppression order relating to the statements and remanded for additional findings of fact and conclusions of law, along with a new hearing if necessary.

While the defendant was being held in jail after his arrest, the decision was made to initiate military discharge proceedings against him. When the defendant was delivered a notice of separation, he signed a memorandum indicating that he would not contest the proceedings. Thereafter and while in jail, he exchanged letters with Schlegelmilch. In the reply letter at issue, the defendant gave an account of the victim's death, including inculpatory statements. The defendant argued that the letter should have been suppressed because it was a response to a letter from Schlegelmilch asking the defendant to explain how the victim had died and thus constituted a custodial interrogation. The court rejected this argument, finding that the circumstances under which the letter was written did not implicate *Miranda*. First, the court noted the defendant's failure to cite any cases supporting the proposition that questioning conducted through an exchange of letters can constitute a custodial interrogation under *Miranda*, nor did the court's own research reveal any legal authority for that proposition. Furthermore, the court noted, when the defendant responded to Schlegelmilch's letter, he was in the midst of being discharged from the military and was not contesting those proceedings, and thus the circumstances "simply do not amount to the type of coercive environment that *Miranda* was intended to address." The court thus affirmed the trial court's denial of the defendant's motion to suppress concerning the letter.

State v. Parlier, 252 N.C. App. 185 (2017). In this child sexual assault case, the court rejected the defendant's argument that his confession was obtained in violation of *Miranda*. During an interview at the sheriff's department, the defendant admitted that he had had sex with the victim. The transcript and videotape of the interview was admitted at trial. The court rejected the defendant's argument that a custodial interrogation occurred. The defendant contacted a detective investigating the case and voluntarily traveled to the sheriff's department. After the detective invited the defendant to speak with her, the defendant followed her to an interview room. The defendant was not handcuffed or restrained, and the interview room door and hallway doors were unlocked. The defendant neither asked to leave nor expressed any reservations about speaking with the detective. A reasonable person in the defendant's position would not have understood this to be a custodial interrogation.

State v. Portillo, 247 N.C. App. 834 (2016). The defendant was injured when, in the course of robbing and murdering a victim, the victim shot back and wounded the defendant. He was taken to the hospital where he remained under officers' guard. The next day, investigators arrived to question him. He made incriminating statements that he later moved to suppress based on the fact that he had not been read his *Miranda* rights. The court of appeals determined that he was not in custody for *Miranda* purposes. His movement was restrained primarily by his medical condition rather than by the police, and he had not been arrested or even handcuffed. The fact that officers suspected him of the crime and may have intended to arrest him was not dispositive.

State v. Barnes, 248 N.C. App. 388, 391 (2016). While the defendant was at his cousin's house, the cousin's parole officer came to the home to conduct a warrantless search of the residence incident to the cousin's parole status. When the parole officer recognized the defendant as a probationer as well, he told him that he was also subject to a search based on his status. The officer put the two men in handcuffs "for officer safety" and seated them on the front porch while he and police officers conducted a search. During the search, the parole officer found a jacket with what appeared to be crack cocaine inside a pocket. The officer asked the defendant and his cousin to identify the owner of the jacket. The defendant claimed the jacket and was charged with a drug offense. The court held that although the defendant was in handcuffs at the time of the questioning, he was not, based on the totality of the circumstances, "in custody" for purposes of *Miranda*. The court stated that "[b]ased on the totality of circumstances, we conclude that a reasonable person in Defendant's situation, though in handcuffs would *not* believe his restraint rose to the level of the restraint associated with a formal arrest." The court noted that the regular conditions of probation include the requirement that a probationer submit to warrantless searches. Also, the defendant was informed that he would be placed in handcuffs for officer safety and was never told that his detention was anything other than temporary. Further, the court reasoned, "as a probationer subject to random searches as a condition of probation, Defendant would objectively understand the purpose of the restraints and the fact that the period of restraint was for a temporary duration." For a more complete discussion of *Barnes*, see Bob Farb, *Court of Appeals Rules That Probationer Was Not in Custody When Handcuffed for Safety Reasons*, UNC SCH. OF GOV'T: N.C. CRIM. L. BLOG (July 26, 2016), https://nccriminallaw.sog.unc.edu/court-appeals-rules-probationer-not-custody-handcuffed-safety-reasons/.

Traffic Cases (page 643)
NORTH CAROLINA COURT OF APPEALS (page 645)

State v. Burris, 253 N.C. App. 525 (2017). The court ruled that the defendant was not in custody for *Miranda* purposes just because an officer had detained him and was in possession of his license. The matter arose when a detective responded to a suspicious person call at a hotel and found the defendant in the driver's seat of a vehicle parked under an overhang. The detective smelled an odor of alcohol and was also concerned about similarities to a robbery that had recently occurred at a nearby hotel. Accordingly, he asked the defendant for identification, then held the defendant's license and instructed the defendant to "hold tight." During the resulting detention, the defendant admitted to driving the vehicle, a fact that became important when he was eventually charged with DWI. He moved to suppress statements he made during that detention, arguing that he had been subjected to custodial interrogation without being given his *Miranda* warnings. Both the trial judge and the court of appeals disagreed, with the latter noting that the defendant had erroneously conflated the *Miranda* custody standard (whether the suspect has been restrained to a degree associated with an arrest) with the standard for a seizure (whether the suspect is free to leave). Here, the defendant was standing outside of his own vehicle while speaking with the detective. He was not handcuffed or told that he was under arrest, and other than his license being retained, his movement was not stopped or limited further. No mention of any possible suspicion of the defendant being involved in criminal activity, impaired driving or otherwise, had yet been made. A reasonable person in these circumstances would not have believed that he or she was under arrest at the time.

The Meaning of "Interrogation" under *Miranda* (page 650)
Generally (page 650)
NORTH CAROLINA COURT OF APPEALS (page 652)

State v. Gamez, 264 N.C. App. 467, 489 (2019) (footnote omitted). The defendant, a U.S. Army private, was charged with second-degree murder, aiding and abetting a first-degree kidnapping, and conspiracy to kidnap. Concerning the defendant's oral statement made to Schlegelmilch, a non-commissioned first sergeant in the U.S. Army, the court vacated and remanded, finding that the trial court (1) did not make factual findings on several issues integral to the question of whether a *Miranda* violation had occurred and (2) failed to fully apply the correct legal standard applicable to the issue. The defendant argued that because he was interrogated by a superior officer who had the power to arrest him, a custodial interrogation occurred. The State countered that no custodial arrest can occur unless the soldier is questioned by a commissioned officer with independent arrest authority. Citing federal law, the court noted that a commanding officer may delegate arrest authority to a non-commissioned officer. When this has occurred, the non-commissioned officer's interrogation of the soldier can trigger the need for *Miranda* warnings. Here, it is undisputed that Schlegelmilch was a non-commissioned officer. Therefore, to resolve the issue of whether the defendant was entitled to *Miranda* warnings, it was necessary to determine whether Schlegelmilch previously had been delegated authority to arrest the defendant by a commanding officer as authorized by federal law. However, the trial court did not make any findings as to whether such a delegation occurred. Additionally, the trial court's order suggests that it failed to understand the potential applicability of *Miranda* if Schlegelmilch had, in fact, been delegated authority to arrest and then proceeded to question the defendant under circumstances amounting to custodial interrogation. Nor did the trial court make findings about the specific degree to which the defendant's liberty had been restricted when he made the statements. The court thus vacated the portion of the trial court's suppression order relating to the statements and remanded for additional findings of fact and conclusions of law, along with a new hearing if necessary.

While the defendant was being held in jail after his arrest, the decision was made to initiate military discharge proceedings against him. When the defendant was delivered a notice of separation, he signed a memorandum indicating that he would not contest the proceedings. Thereafter and while in jail, he exchanged letters with Schlegelmilch. In the reply letter at issue, the defendant gave an account of the victim's death, including inculpatory statements. The defendant argued that the letter should have been suppressed because it was a response to a letter from Schlegelmilch asking the defendant to explain how the victim had died and thus constituted a custodial interrogation. The court rejected this argument, finding that the circumstances under which the letter was written did not implicate *Miranda*. First, the court noted the defendant's failure to cite any cases supporting the proposition that questioning conducted through an exchange of letters can constitute a custodial interrogation under *Miranda*, nor did the court's own research reveal any legal authority for that proposition. Furthermore, the court noted, when the defendant responded to Schlegelmilch's letter, he was in the midst of being discharged from the military and was not contesting those proceedings, and thus the circumstances "simply do not amount to the type of coercive environment that *Miranda* was intended to address." The court thus affirmed the trial court's denial of the defendant's motion to suppress concerning the letter.

FEDERAL APPELLATE COURTS (page 655)

United States v. Bell, 901 F.3d 455, 460, 462, 463, 464 (4th Cir. 2018). The defendant was convicted at trial of various drugs and firearms offenses in federal district court and appealed, arguing that the trial judge improperly denied his motions to suppress a statement and to reveal the identity of the confidential informant in the case, among other evidentiary and sentencing issues. A task force from the U.S. Bureau of Alcohol, Tobbaco, Firearms and Explosives (ATF) raided the defendant's residence pursuant to a search warrant that was supported in part by an informant's statements. According to the search warrant affidavit, the informant told the ATF agents that large amounts of heroin were being stored in and sold from the defendant's residence. The informant claimed to have been to the residence recently and to have seen distribution quantities of drugs, as well as a firearm, and was able to identify the defendant. When agents entered the home, they cuffed the defendant and ultimately sat him in a chair beside his wife (who was actually the sole owner of the home). An agent approached the wife, informed her of the search warrant, and asked if there were any weapons in the home that might hurt the officers. Before his wife responded, the defendant volunteered that "there was a gun under the couch" and that "a friend had given him the gun . . ." A semiautomatic rifle was found under the couch, and substantial amounts of drugs, cash, and drug-distribution paraphernalia were discovered throughout the home.

The defendant filed motions to have his statement about the presence of the gun suppressed as a *Miranda* violation and to have the identity of the informant disclosed, both of which were denied by the trial judge. The defendant's suppression argument focused on whether the questioning of his wife in his presence constituted an "interrogation" for purposes of *Miranda*. *Miranda* warnings are required whenever a suspect is in custody and subject to interrogation. Interrogation can consist of "express questioning or its *functional equivalent*." Under *Rhode Island v. Innis*, 446 U.S. 291, 301 (1980), "words or actions on the part of the police . . . that the police should know are reasonably likely to elicit an incriminating response" can constitute interrogation for *Miranda* purposes. The fourth circuit concluded that the agent's question to the defendant's wife did not rise to the level of direct interrogation or its functional equivalent:

> Agent Oliver focused directly on [the wife] as the owner of the house, looked her in the eye, and asked a single question relating to officer safety—whether there were any weapons in the house that would hurt an officer. The question was not posed to the defendant and did not seek a response from him, nor was there any evidence that it was intended to.

That the defendant was married to his wife and sat nearby at the time was not enough to presume the agent should have known his question would prompt the defendant's response. The *Innis* "functional equivalent" standard was simply not met here without some other coercive action by the police, above and beyond the fact that the defendant was in custody. "It can hardly be said that overhearing a single question posed to one's spouse creates the necessary level of compulsion without more." The court therefore affirmed the denial of the motion to suppress, finding that the defendant fell "well short" of establishing that his statement was coerced.

United States v. Oloyede, 933 F.3d 302, 308, 309 (4th Cir. 2019) (internal quotation marks, citations omitted). In this multi-defendant wire fraud case in federal district court, one defendant moved to suppress evidence obtained from her cell phone. While police were executing a search warrant at her home, an agent discovered a locked cell phone in this defendant's bedroom. He asked the defendant, "Could you please unlock your iPhone?" The defendant then unlocked the phone and gave it back to the agent. Her motion to suppress the contents of her phone alleged that this was a Fifth Amendment violation of her right to remain silent, and that she should have been Mirandized before the request. The district court rejected this argument, finding that the act of unlocking her phone was not a communication subject to *Miranda*. It further found that the agent's request was not "coercive" and that the defendant voluntarily complied. The fourth circuit affirmed. The Fifth Amendment protection from self-incrimination applies to compelled testimonial communications that inculpate the defendant. A testimonial communication may consist of an act, but "the act must 'relate a factual assertion or disclose information,' . . . ; it must 'express the contents of [the person's] mind.' " Here, the agent did not ask the defendant for the password; he asked her to enter it herself. The defendant did not show the agent the password, and the agent did not see it when the defendant entered it to unlock the phone. "Unlike a circumstance, for instance, in which she gave the passcode to the agent for the agent to enter, here she simply used the unexpressed contents of her mind to type the passcode herself." This act did not qualify as a testimonial communication and was unprotected by the Fifth Amendment. Furthermore, even if the defendant's act of unlocking her phone did constitute a testimonial communication, the phone would still have been admissible: "[T]he *Miranda* rule is a prophylactic employed to protect against violations of the Self-Incrimination Clause and . . . the Clause 'is not implicated by the admission into evidence of the physical fruit of a voluntary statement.' " This situation fell within the rule set out in *United States v. Patane*, 542 U.S. 630 (2004), which the fourth circuit cited, in that use of the phone evidence at trial did not create any risk that coerced statements by the defendant would be used at trial. The court affirmed the trial court's denial of the defendant's motion to suppress.

Volunteered Statements (page 655)

NORTH CAROLINA COURT OF APPEALS (page 656)

State v. Moore, 254 N.C. App. 544, 569 (2017). The trial court did not err by denying the defendant's motion to suppress statements made to an officer while the officer was transporting the defendant to the law enforcement center. It was undisputed that the defendant made the inculpatory statements while in custody and before he had been given his *Miranda* rights. However, the court held that the defendant was not subjected to interrogation; rather, his statements were spontaneous utterances. This was so even though the statements followed a supervising officer's radio communication with the transporting officer in which the supervisor asked the transporting officer whether the defendant had said anything about the location of the vehicle involved in the incident. This "brief exchange between two law enforcement officers" was not directed at the defendant, was not the functional equivalent of an interrogation, and did not call for an incriminating response.

State v. Burton, 251 N.C. App. 600 (2017). The defendant and another man were arrested in connection with the possession of marijuana and cocaine in a vehicle. The arresting officer obtained charges against both individuals, then read the arrest warrants to each arrestee in the other's presence. The defendant told the officer that the other individual should not be charged with possession of the cocaine because it was the defendant's. That statement was not obtained in violation of *Miranda*—reading the arrest warrants aloud was not "interrogation." Arresting officers must inform arrestees of the charges against them, and the defendant failed to show that reading the charges in the presence of both arrestees was designed to elicit an incriminating response.

Evidentiary Use of a Defendant's Silence or Assertion of Right to Counsel or Right to Remain Silent (page 676)

NORTH CAROLINA COURT OF APPEALS (page 678)

State v. Shuler, ___ N.C. App. ___, 841 S.E.2d 607 (2020). Officers were called about a disturbance at a hotel involving a specific car. They arrived and approached the vehicle. A man standing outside of the car identified himself, officers quickly determined there were outstanding warrants for his arrest, and he was taken into custody. Officers approached the defendant, who was seated in the car. She, too, had outstanding warrants. Before one of the officers took her into custody, he asked if she had any contraband. The defendant silently removed a bag of marijuana from her bra in response. The officer then asked if she had any more contraband, specifically asking about methamphetamines, and explained that possession of drugs in jail is a separate charge. The defendant again silently removed another bag (this time, of methamphetamine) from her bra. She was arrested and charged with trafficking methamphetamine and possession of marijuana. Before trial, the defendant gave notice of intent to rely on duress as a defense. She alleged that the man standing beside the car (with whom she admitted associating) threw the drugs at her as police arrived and threatened to "chain her to a tree" if she didn't hide them.

At trial, an officer on the scene was asked by the State during its case-in-chief whether the defendant made any statements about the man standing by the car at the time of her arrest. The defense objected on Fifth Amendment grounds and was overruled. The defendant then moved for a mistrial outside the presence of the jury and again complained that the State's question emphasized the defendant's silence at the time of arrest. This motion was denied. The defendant testified about the alleged duress but did not explain her silence at the time of police questioning. On appeal, the defendant renewed her Fifth Amendment objections to the officer testimony about her silence.

While it is improper for the State to use a defendant's silence following arrest as substantive evidence of guilt, the evidence may be admissible for impeachment when a defendant's prior silence is inconsistent with his or her present statements at trial. The defendant here argued that her testimony was improperly used as substantive evidence of guilt, arising from the State's effort to preempt her duress defense. The defendant relied on *State v. Mendoza*, 206 N.C. App. 391 (2010), when the court found error based on this type of preemptive impeachment evidence concerning the defendant's pre-arrest silence. The court here distinguished that case and found that because the defendant gave notice of intent to rely on duress, she could be preemptively impeached with evidence of her pre-arrest silence.

When the State seeks to impeach a defendant through silence, the test for admissibility of the defendant's testimony is whether, under the circumstances at the time of arrest, it would have been natural for the defendant to have asserted the same defense asserted at trial. Here, it would have been natural for a defendant to have told the arresting officer that the contraband she possessed belonged to the other man and that he had threatened her to conceal it, if she believed that to be the case. The admission of this testimony was therefore not error.

State v. Perry, 260 N.C. App. 659, 662–63 (2018). The court ruled that the trial court did not err by allowing the prosecutor to cross-examine defendant Perry regarding his post-arrest, pre-*Miranda* silence. Defendants Perry and Powell appealed from judgments entered upon jury verdicts finding them guilty of offenses in connection with a shooting. The defendants were tried together. At trial, Perry testified regarding his alibi defense. On appeal, the defendants argued that the trial court committed reversible error by allowing the prosecutor to cross-examine Perry about his silence to the police after his arrest regarding his alibi. Although a defendant's post-arrest, post-*Miranda* warning silence may not be used by the State for any purpose, a defendant's post-arrest, pre-*Miranda* silence may be used by the State to impeach a defendant by suggesting that the defendant's prior silence is inconsistent with his or her present statements at trial. The court noted that the North Carolina Supreme Court has instructed that a defendant's silence about an alibi at the time of arrest can constitute an inconsistent statement and that this silence can be used to impeach an alibi offered by the defendant at trial if it would have been natural for the defendant to mention the alibi at the time of his or her encounter with the police. Applying these rules to the case at hand, the court concluded:

> [T]here was evidence which showed as follows: The offenses were perpetrated no more than 72 hours before Defendant Perry was arrested and informed of the charges against him. Defendant Perry knew the victims named in the warrant: he knew one of the victims because she was his ex-girlfriend, and he knew the other victim from hanging out in the same neighborhood. Despite Defendant Perry's familiarity with these two victims and the location where the shooting occurred, he made no statements that he had an alibi to account for his whereabouts during the commission of the crime. When the officer charged Defendant Perry with three counts of attempted murder and three counts of injury to real or personal property, Defendant Perry failed to mention his alibi when it would have been natural to deny that he would not have attempted to kill his ex-girlfriend, her current partner, and his ex-girlfriend's son.

> Based on this evidence, we conclude that Defendant Perry's silence is inconsistent with his later alibi testimony presented for the first time during trial. Therefore, the trial court did not err when it allowed the State to impeach Defendant Perry on cross-examination about his failure to say anything about his alibi when the warrants were read to him and before he had received *Miranda* warnings.

Although it was error to admit evidence of Perry's post-*Miranda* warnings silence about an alibi, the error did not constitute plain error for either defendant. Because Perry failed to object to the testimony at trial, the plain error standard applied. Here, no plain error occurred because there was ample evidence establishing the defendants' guilt.

North Carolina Statutory Warnings for Young Arrestees (page 684)

NORTH CAROLINA SUPREME COURT (page 684)

State v. Saldierna, 369 N.C. 401, 409 (2016). Officers arrested a 16-year-old juvenile in connection with several break-ins and sought to question him. The juvenile was advised of, and signed a waiver of, his *Miranda* rights and his statutory right to have a parent or guardian present during questioning. Shortly thereafter, he asked, "Um, can I call my mom?" An officer allowed him to use a phone, but he was unable to reach his mother. The interview resumed, and the juvenile admitted involvement in the break-ins. He later moved to suppress statements he made during the interview, contending that his request to call his mother amounted to an assertion of his right to have a parent present. The motion was denied by the trial judge. The court of appeals reversed, concluding that the question was ambiguous but that, unlike in the *Miranda* context, an officer should clarify ambiguous comments regarding juvenile rights. The state supreme court reversed again, ruling that the juvenile's remark was "at best an ambiguous invocation of his right to have his mother present" and applying *Miranda* precedent in holding that "without an unambiguous, unequivocal invocation of defendant's right [to have a parent or guardian present] law enforcement officers had no duty to ask clarifying questions or to cease questioning." The court remanded the matter to the court of appeals to review whether the juvenile's waiver of his rights was knowing and voluntary. For a more complete discussion of *Saldierna*, see Bob Farb, *North Carolina Supreme Court Rules That Juvenile's Request to Call Mother During Custodial Interrogation Was Not Clear Invocation of Statutory Right to Consult a Parent or Guardian to Bar Further Interrogation*, UNC Sch. of Gov't: N.C. Crim. L. Blog (Feb. 28, 2017), https://nccriminallaw.sog.unc.edu/north-carolina-supreme-court-rules-juveniles-request-call-mother-custodial-interrogation-not-clear-invocation-statutory-right-consult-parent-guardian-bar-furt/.

In later litigation, *State v. Saldierna*, 371 N.C. 407 (2018), involving the defendant's case (see summary above), the court, reversing the court of appeals, 254 N.C. App. 446 (2017), ruled that the evidence supported the trial judge's finding that the juvenile knowingly and voluntarily waived his juvenile rights.

NORTH CAROLINA COURT OF APPEALS (page 684)

State v. Benitez, 258 N.C. App. 491, 514 (2018). The 13-year-old defendant was questioned by a detective in the presence of his uncle, with whom he lived, and admitted shooting a victim in the head. Two weeks later, the court appointed the county department of social services as a guardian for the defendant because he had appeared in court with no family, his mother was believed to be in El Salvador, and his father's whereabouts were unknown. The defendant eventually pled guilty to first-degree murder and later filed a motion for appropriate relief, alleging that his trial counsel had provided ineffective assistance by failing to move to suppress the statement he made to the detective as obtained in violation of the defendant's statutory right to have a parent or guardian present during questioning. The attorney indicated that he had researched the issue but concluded that the uncle qualified as a guardian under existing case law given that the juvenile had lived with him for more than a year, that he met the juvenile's needs, and that he signed paperwork for school and otherwise as the defendant's guardian. Although *State v. Oglesby*, 361 N.C. 550 (2007) (finding that a juvenile's aunt was not a guardian and stating that only a "legal process" could render a person a guardian), was perhaps to the contrary, the precise scope and meaning of *Oglesby* was not clear at the time and counsel's decision not to pursue the issue based on the research he had done was not unreasonable. As a second issue, the defendant argued that his waiver of his right to remain silent was not knowing, voluntary, and intelligent. The court of appeals remanded that issue for further findings by the trial court, noting a lack of findings regarding the defendant's "experience, education, background, and intelligence." The court appeared to be especially concerned with suggestions in the record that the defendant suffered from some mental disease or defect, perhaps an intellectual disability.

Scope of Fifth Amendment Privilege of a Defendant or Witness at Trial (page 702)

NORTH CAROLINA SUPREME COURT (page 704)

State v. Diaz, 372 N.C. 493 (2019). The court ruled that the trial judge erred by admitting the defendant's affidavit of indigency into evidence over the defendant's objection to show his age, which was an element of the charged crimes in this abduction of a child and statutory rape case. The trial judge had ruled that the affidavit of indigency was admissible under Rule 902 of the N.C. Rules of Evidence as a self-authenticating document, but the supreme court concluded that allowing the document into evidence impermissibly compelled the defendant to surrender one constitutional right—his Fifth Amendment right against self-incrimination—in order to complete the paperwork required for him to assert his Sixth Amendment right to the assistance of counsel as an indigent defendant. However, the court also ruled that, based on the facts in this case, the trial judge's error was harmless beyond a reasonable doubt.

II. Lineups and Other Identification Procedures (page 709)

Due Process Review of Identification Procedures (page 710)

Generally (page 710)

NORTH CAROLINA SUPREME COURT (page 711)

State v. Malone, 373 N.C. 134, 148, 149 (2019). The court ruled that identifications by two eyewitnesses to a shooting committed by two suspects were tainted by a trial preparation meeting between the two eyewitnesses and a legal assistant from the district attorney's office.

The eyewitnesses viewed photo lineups two days after the shooting. The two women identified one of the suspects, who was not the defendant. However, they were unable to identify the other suspect, the defendant, who was tried and convicted as the other person involved in the shooting. For three and a half years the eyewitnesses had no contact with the State until the legal assistant met them at the courthouse for trial preparation. She showed them the defendant's recorded interview with officers and photos of the defendant. One of the women looked out the window and saw the defendant, in a jail uniform and handcuffs, being led into the courthouse for a hearing. She immediately stated that he was one of the killers. The other woman came to the window and also saw the defendant. Both women later identified the defendant at trial as one of the perpetrators.

The court ruled that the trial preparation session was an "impermissibly suggestive" identification procedure. Given that the women had not previously identified the defendant as a participant in the crime, the legal assistant's "actions in showing [the women] the video of [the defendant's] interview and recent photographs . . . are exactly the kind of highly suggestive procedures that have been widely condemned as inherently suggestive" and amounted to improper witness coaching. However, the court found that the procedure did not give "rise to a substantial likelihood of irreparable misidentification . . . because the trial court's findings of fact support the legal conclusion that [one of the women's] in-court identification of defendant was of independent origin and sufficiently reliable." Among other factors, the court highlighted the woman's proximity to the perpetrators, her opportunity to observe them, and the fact that when she saw a picture of the defendant online shortly after the crime—wearing his hair in a style different from his lineup photo and apparently more similar to his appearance at the time of the crime—she identified him as a perpetrator. Because one of the women made a valid in-court identification, any error in admitting the other woman's in-court identification of the defendant was harmless beyond a reasonable doubt.

NORTH CAROLINA COURT OF APPEALS (page 712)

State v. Juene, 263 N.C. App. 543, 545–46 (2019). The court ruled that the trial court did not err by denying the defendant's motion to suppress evidence which asserted that the pre-trial identification was impermissibly suggestive. Three victims were robbed in a mall parking lot by three assailants. The defendant was apprehended and identified by the victims as one of the perpetrators. The defendant unsuccessfully moved to suppress the show-up identification made by the victims. On appeal, the defendant argued that the show-up identification should have been suppressed because it was impermissibly suggestive. Before the robbery occurred, the defendant and the other perpetrators followed the victims around the mall and the parking lot. The defendant was two feet from one of the victims at the time of the robbery. The show-up occurred approximately fifteen minutes after the crime. Before the show-up, the victims gave a physical description of the defendant to law enforcement. All three victims were seated together in the back of a police car during the show-up. The defendant and the other perpetrators were handcuffed during the show-up and standing in a well-lit area of the parking lot in front of the police car. The defendant matched the description given by the victims. When approaching the area where the defendant and the others were detained, all three victims spontaneously shouted, "That's him, that's him"; and all of the victims identified the defendant in court. Although these procedures "were not perfect," there was not a substantial likelihood of misidentification in light of the reliability factors surrounding the crime and the identification. "Even though the show-up may have been suggestive, it did not rise to the level of irreparable misidentification."

State v. Pless, 263 N.C. App. 341, 348 (2018). The court ruled that the trial court did not err by denying the defendant's motion to suppress evidence concerning in-court identifications which the defendant asserted were unreliable because they were tainted by an impermissibly suggestive DMV photograph. Detective Jurney conducted an undercover drug purchase from a man known as Junior, who arrived at the agreed-upon location in a gold Lexus. A surveillance team, including Sergeant Walker, witnessed the transaction. Junior's true identity was unknown at the time, but Walker obtained the defendant's name from a confidential informant. Several days after the transaction, Walker obtained a photograph of the defendant from the DMV and showed it to Jurney. Walker testified that he had seen the defendant on another occasion driving the same vehicle with the same license plate number as the one used during the drug transaction. At trial, Jurney and Walker identified the defendant as the person who sold the drugs in the undercover purchase.

The defendant argued on appeal that the trial court erred by failing to address whether the identification was impermissibly suggestive. The court found that although the trial court did not make an explicit conclusion of law that the identification procedure was not impermissibly suggestive, it is clear that the trial court implicitly so concluded. The court found the defendant's cited cases distinguishable, noting in part that there is no absolute prohibition on using a single photograph for an identification. The court noted that even if the trial court failed to conclude that the identification procedure was not impermissibly suggestive, it did not err in its alternative conclusion that the identification was reliable under the totality of the circumstances. It concluded:

> While we recognize that it is the better practice to use multiple photos in a photo identification procedure, the trial court did not err in its conclusion that, in this case, the use of a single photo was not impermissibly suggestive. And even if the procedure was impermissibly suggestive, the trial court's findings of fact also support a conclusion that the procedure did not create "a substantial likelihood of irreparable misidentification." The trial court's findings of fact in this order are supported by competent evidence, and these factual findings support the trial court's ultimate conclusions of law.

State v. Mitchell, 262 N.C. App. 344 (2018). The court ruled that the trial court properly denied the defendant's motion to suppress a victim's identification of the defendant as the perpetrator of a robbery. The defendant was charged with armed robbery of a Game Stop store and with threatening the use of a firearm against a store employee, Cintron, during the robbery. Although Cintron failed to identify an alleged perpetrator in a photographic lineup shown to him two days after the robbery, he later identified the defendant when shown a single still-frame photograph obtained from the store's surveillance video. Cintron then identified the defendant as the perpetrator in the same photographic lineup shown to him two days after the robbery and again in four close-up, post-arrest photographs of the defendant showing his neck tattoos. The defendant unsuccessfully moved to suppress Cintron's in-court and out-of-court identifications.

On appeal, the defendant argued that the State conducted an impermissibly suggestive pretrial identification procedure that created a substantial likelihood of misidentification. The court rejected that argument, finding that the trial court's challenged findings and conclusions—that the authorities substantially followed statutory and police department policies in each photo lineup and that the substance of any deviation from those policies revolved around the defendant's neck tattoos—were supported by the evidence. The defendant fit the victim's initial description of the perpetrator, which emphasized a tattoo of an Asian symbol on the left side of his neck and notable forehead creases. Based on this description, the victim had the ability to identify the defendant both in court and in photographs reflecting a close-up view of the defendant's tattoos, and he specifically testified to his ability to recognize the defendant as the perpetrator independent of any lineup or photo he had been shown. Thus, the trial court's ultimate conclusion—that the procedures did not give rise to a substantial likelihood that the defendant was mistakenly identified—was supported by the totality of the circumstances indicating that the identification was sufficiently reliable.

Statutory Procedures Involving Lineups (page 714)

NORTH CAROLINA COURT OF APPEALS (page 714)

State v. Reaves-Smith, ___ N.C. App. ___, 844 S.E.2d 19 (2020). Two men attempted to rob the victim in a McDonald's parking lot. One of the suspects fired a gun, and both suspects fled. The victim ran to a nearby parking lot, where he found a law enforcement officer. The victim told the officer what had occurred and described the suspects. Two suspects matching the description were located nearby a few minutes later. When officers approached, the defendant ran. He was apprehended a few minutes later. The victim was taken to the location where the defendant was apprehended, and the victim identified the defendant as the person with a gun who had tried to rob him earlier. The identification was recorded on one of the officer's body cameras.

The defendant was indicted for attempted robbery with a dangerous weapon. He moved to suppress the victim's show-up identification. The trial court denied the motion, and the defendant was convicted at trial. The defendant appealed, arguing that the trial court erred when it denied his motion to suppress evidence of the show-up identification and when it failed to instruct the jury about purported noncompliance with the North Carolina Eyewitness Identification Reform Act (the Act).

The court noted that G.S. 15A-284.52(c1), the section of the Act covering show-up procedures, provides that

- "A show-up may only be conducted when a suspect matching the description of the perpetrator is located in close proximity in time and place to the crime, or there is reasonable belief that the perpetrator has changed his or her appearance in close time to the crime, and only if there are circumstances that require the immediate display of a suspect to an eyewitness";
- A show-up may only be performed using a live suspect; and
- Investigators must photograph a suspect at the time and place of the show-up in order to preserve a record of the suspect's appearance at the time of the show-up.

The court determined that the trial court made findings that supported each of these requirements. The defendant, who matched the victim's description, was detained less than a half-mile from the site of the attempted robbery. He was suspected of a violent crime that involved the discharge of a firearm and fled when officers first attempted to detain him. These circumstances required an immediate display of the defendant.

An armed suspect who is not detained poses an imminent threat to the public. Had the victim determined that the defendant was not the perpetrator, officers could have released the defendant and continued their search. Finally, the show-up involved a live suspect and was recorded on camera.

The court rejected the defendant's argument that the Act requires law enforcement officers to obtain a confidence statement and information related to the victim's vision. G.S. 15A-284.52(c2) requires the North Carolina Criminal Justice Education and Training Standards Commission to develop a policy regarding standard procedures for show-ups. According to the statute, the policy must address "[c]onfidence statements by the eyewitness, including information related to the eyewitness' vision, the circumstances of the events witnessed, and communications with other eyewitnesses, if any." The court reasoned that because G.S. 15A-284.52(c2) does not place additional statutory requirements on law enforcement but instead requires the North Carolina Criminal Justice Education and Training Standards Commission to develop non-binding guidelines, only G.S. 15A-284.52(c1) sets forth the requirements for show-up identification compliance.

The court further determined that the show-up here did not violate the defendant's due process rights as it was not impermissibly suggestive and did not create a substantial likelihood of misidentification.

G.S. 15A-284.52(d)(3) provides that when evidence of compliance or noncompliance with "this section" of the Act is presented at trial, the jury must be instructed that it may consider credible evidence of compliance or noncompliance to determine the reliability of eyewitness identifications. The defendant argued on appeal that he was entitled to a jury instruction on noncompliance with the Act because the officer did not obtain an eyewitness confidence statement as required under G.S. 15A-284.52(c2)(2). The court rejected that argument on the basis that G.S. 15A-284.52(c2) concerns policies and guidelines established by the North Carolina Criminal Justice Education and Training Standards Commission, not the requirements for show-up identifications. Because the officers complied with the show-up procedures in G.S. 15A-284.52(c1), the defendant was not entitled to a jury instruction on noncompliance with the Act.

State v. Crumitie, ___ N.C. App. ___, 831 S.E.2d 592 (2019). An officer responded to a shooting at the victim's apartment. Upon arrival, he saw a man running with a towel in his hands and gave chase. The officer could not catch the man and instead found one of the victims, the defendant's ex-girlfriend. She was able to describe the assailant and provide his name. The officer then located a DMV picture of the suspect and identified the defendant as the person he saw running earlier. The defendant sought to suppress this identification as a violation of the North Carolina Eyewitness Identification Reform Act (the Act). Specifically, the defendant argued that the officer failed to conduct the "show-up" in accord with the procedure required under the Act. The trial court denied the motion, and the court of appeals affirmed. The Act applies to "live lineups, photo lineups, and show-ups." Here, the court stated, the inadvertent out-of-court identification of the defendant, based on one DMV photo accessed by the investigating officer, was neither a lineup nor a show-up under the Act, and thus not subject to the statute's protections. Even if the identification was suggestive, there was no substantial likelihood of misidentification under the facts of the case, and the denial of the motion was affirmed.

On page 715, the main volume summarizes *State v. Boozer.* The correct citation for that case is 210 N.C. App. 371 (2011), not 210 N.C. App. 391 (2011).

Case and Statute Index

Note: United States Supreme Court cases are in **bold**.

Cases

Statutes